Be Yourself

Evolving the World
Through Personal Empowerment

by Mark Gilbert

Be Yourself:
Evolving the World Through Personal Empowerment

Copyright © 2012 by Mark Gilbert

All rights reserved.

No part of this book may be reproduced, scanned, or distributed in any printed or electronic form without permission. Please do not participate in or encourage piracy of copyrighted material in violation of the author's rights. Purchase only authorized editions.

Publisher: Conscious Bridge Publishing

ISBN: 978-0-9883032-0-1

Library of Congress Control Number: 2012919785

Book and Cover Design: Gary D. Hall,
 Greystroke Creative
Editorial Services: Alexi Paulina

Printed in the United States of America

Copies of this book may be ordered from:

www.amazon.com
http://consciousbridge.com

Contents

Foreword

Introduction

Part One: Our Current Evolutionary Crossroads • 1
    A Humble Theory of Our Evolution. 3
    The Challenge. 15
    The Bridge to Our Future 23

Part Two: Focusing Upon Our Commonalities • 27
    A Brief List of Human Common Characteristics 29
    Born into the Human Story. 33
    Living in Two Worlds. 51
    Directing Consciousness 65

Part Three: Visions of Our Highest Future • 77
    Scientists, Philosophers and Mystics Ideas About
        Evolution's Direction 79
    Common Themes 103
    A Compelling Common Vision?. 105

Part Four: Becoming Yourself • 117
    Identifying and Answering Your Calling 119
    Letting Go of Limitations. 131
    Becoming Your True Self...and Serving Others 143

Part Five: Moving Forward in Your Life • 155
    Putting the Theory Into Practice 157
    Our Humble Theory Revisited 161

Bibliography and Resources • 167

United Nations Millennium Declaration • 169

About the Author • 185

Notes • 187

Foreword

Although I grew up in the Gandhi family where Gandhi's philosophy was practiced assiduously I did not buy into it wholly. As an adult I found myself caught in the trap of materialism, ambition and unreasonable expectations of others that it began to affect my health. After I passed fifty my blood pressure shot up, I paid less and less attention to my health all because I was told these are normal occurrences in old age. In other words I was not being myself. I believed success depends entirely on latching on to your dream, however unreasonable, working hard to reach impossible goals, setting inordinately high expectations not only from myself but from friends and colleagues as well. All that mattered to me was me and my ambition and the hope of attaining it by any means possible. I bought into the way of life that a materialistic society promotes.

Then one day I began to reflect on grandfather's theory of non-attachment—as distinct from detachment. In non-attachment you don't give up your dreams, family and friends altogether but you are no longer attached to them. On the other hand in detachment the implication is that you detach yourself completely and let go. That could be the final stage of an ascetic's life.

I saw the wisdom in non-attachment and began to let go of my expectations and ambitions and gladly accepted the fruits of sincere labor, whatever they were. It made an amazing impact on my health. My blood pressure came down to normal and I had time and inclination to care for my health in general. It woke me to the fact that there is more to life than making money and controlling family and friends. The Rev. Mark Gilbert gives us many pointers in his book so that we find the time to "smell the roses" and enjoy the pleasures of living that money cannot buy. I recommend this book whole-heartedly.

—Arun Gandhi
President, Gandhi Worldwide Education Institute
www.gandhiforchildren.org

Introduction

You've opened this book and are curious what it's about.

Simply stated, it's about you. It's about you becoming and living fully as the person you came into this life to be. The irony is that in living that life, you don't become selfish and egocentric. Rather, what I hope you recognize is that in living on purpose, you actually become more selfless and "world-centric." In serving yourself and meeting your own highest needs, you synchronistically meet the needs of others.

I recognize that sounds very altruistic, and maybe some part of it resonates with you—but maybe some part doesn't. In truth, we all have a selfish side. Life has taught us the importance of looking out for our own needs. I want to fulfill my desires, and I know you want to fulfill yours.

This book also is about love –not love in the popularized sense presented to us in movies, music, and romance novels, but love as a force inspiring us to grow.

We all have experienced love in our lives; that feeling is part of the force I'm talking about. Recalling that feeling in moments with our lovers, friends, family, children, and pets gives us an inkling of how this power of love seeks to connect us with something outside of us. Here's a quick story to give you a sense of the kind of love I'm speaking about.

I remember the first time I saw Harmony. I was living alone in a small duplex, not long after separating from my first wife. My oldest daughter, Melanie, called and asked if she could come over with her brother, Matthew. When they arrived, they were holding a small, chocolate-colored Labrador retriever puppy. She was my birthday present, and it was love at first sight.

Months earlier, at the time my wife and I separated, we had been keeping Melanie's chocolate Lab, Java, while my daughter was out of the country. Java came with me to the small duplex and supported me in a loving way throughout that time of change. In appreciation for her love, I would have let Java stay with me forever, but Melanie obviously wanted her back when she returned to America. It was then that Harmony came into my life and filled the void. I named her that first night, as I saw her as bringing harmony into my life and the lives of others. Years later, I know that she has done just that.

Harmony was my comforter and best friend as I moved through a series of life changes. She was there when I got divorced and began to date. Her wisdom provided counsel as to which relationships were truly in my best interests, and she guided me to Mary. It was the strong bond of love between Harmony and Mary that served as a signpost that ours was to be a committed, long-term relationship.

Harmony has seen me through career changes, moves to new homes, and remarriage. She has filled my life with so much joy, excitedly greeting me each time I come home. At set times each day, she herds me outside to play ball, her passion. Harmony licks my face every time we back out of the driveway when we're going for a ride together. She directs Mary and me to bed each night and then curls up beside us.

There is a deep and unspoken bond between Harmony and me. We read each other's body energy and know exactly what the other needs at that moment. She provides for me, and I provide for her. Although she can't utter spoken words, she generally understands exactly what I am saying.

Each time I look at Harmony, an emotional energy wells up in me and makes me want to scoop her up, hold her, and love on her—to somehow connect the essence of who I am with the essence of who she is at a deeper level. Most of us have had these experiences at times. Mary and I call them "moments to live for," acknowledging that there is an aspect of that experience that we know connects to the true meaning of life.

I have had those moments throughout my life. I can recall times (when I was growing up and when I was first married) when this power ignited within me. I can remember the births of my five children and how I was overcome with love. I can remember the feeling I had when I asked Mary to marry me and she said yes. I can remember seeing my grandchildren for the first time and sensing the wondrous continuity of life, as new generations come into being and love keeps moving us forward. What are those moments in your life?

In recent years, Mary and I sometimes took care of Java for Melanie. Java and Harmony seemed to be soul mates; there was a natural loving nature between the two dogs. Mary came to love Java as I did, recognizing the specialness of her soul. On a recent Christmas Eve, we babysat Java on what we later realized was her last day on earth. Her health had declined; it was difficult for her to stand up and walk. Whenever she needed to go outside, I had to carry her in and out of the house. Yet even in such a compromised state of physical health, Java's essence still was that of the loving creature that had supported me through my time of change and was instrumental in bringing Harmony into my life.

Melanie and her husband picked up Java late in the afternoon. Early on Christmas morning, we heard that she had died during the night. I wept profusely.

We all know that birth, life, and death are the natural cycle of our experience here on Earth. We experience the cycle through our connectedness with others, watching them move through the stages. I don't remember my birth and have not reached the point of my death. Yet, there are those who experienced my birth and those who will experience my ultimate departure from this plane. Our movement through the cycle becomes the experience for others. Experiencing this cycle brings both joy and sorrow. These experiences are part of the reason we are here.

Often, we feel alone. We believe that we are an individual residing inside our body, separate from everyone else "out there." The feeling of love we have for others draws us out from being a "human hermit." It calls us to a sense of connectedness with others. Sometimes, acting upon this force leads us to vulnerable and painful situations such as dealing with death and divorce. Yet, this ultimately is a small price to pay for the joy and bliss we gain when love connects us deeply with another being, even for a short time. Why does love call us out of our shell to connect with others?

In these pages, I will offer you some ideas on this and other topics. These are simply some reflections on the nature of life and why we are here—ideas drawn from my studies and life experiences. They are designed to open you to what may be a new way of looking at life. My hope is that (no matter what your current beliefs are about the meaning of life and why you are here) you will gain some food for thought to incorporate into your viewpoint.

Briefly, I hope you take from this book the following:

that you view your life and all of our lives as part of a developmental process, and see that we all are *evolving*. This evolution is occurring right now in your personal life and in our collective lives. I hope you will consider that you, I, and all of humanity are at a major crossroads in our developmental path. Current planetary crises are presenting us with a choice. One direction appears bleak; the other is positive and hopeful. Which will we choose?

I offer you three keys that I believe will move us toward the positive future. The first is to shift our attention away from our differences and focus on how we are alike. The second is to shift our intentions toward the vision of that highest future. The third key is to recognize your unique and individual talent—the reason you came to the planet—and begin living it wholeheartedly. That "selfish" act is really an act of love. Ultimately, love is leading us along the path to our highest possibilities.

My intention is that the ideas presented here will shift your perspective on life and call you to move through the world a bit differently. We will consider how you might take control of your life, consciously directing your own evolution to become the highest vision of who you can be.

Ultimately, this book is about finding and living the life you were called here to live. It's about being yourself—your true self—at its deepest level. I want you to selfishly move toward that goal.

Some of the following pages may take a global perspective. At times, we will delve into the "big picture" in ways that may not seem relevant to your individual life. I realize that it isn't always easy to feel excited about steering our lives so as to make the planet a better place. What I hope you understand is that directing your life to meet your highest personal needs will serve to improve the planet, even if that was not your direct intention.

I have come to realize (and I hope you do too) that when you truly identify your life's purpose and selfishly pursue it, you can't help but move outside yourself and desire to be of service and in love with all of life. The question then becomes for you, "Where is the best place for humanity to move to, and how can I serve that growth?" That is love in action.

Part One:

Our Current Evolutionary Crossroads

In the first section of the book, we will explore the following ideas:

- You individually and all of humanity are "evolving."
- Much of our early evolution was in the physical realm.
- More recently, our evolution has been occurring in our social structures.
- Our future evolution will take place mainly in our consciousness and the spiritual realm.
- Our current planetary challenges are indicative of a potential crossroads or choice point.
- Through our choices, we hold the key to move toward either a bleak future or a positive one.
- There are three keys to moving toward our highest future.
- The first key is for each of us to shift our attention away from our differences and toward the things we share.

- The second key is for each of us to focus our attention toward a vision of the greatest possibilities for the future.
- The third key is for each of us to fully answer our calling and do all we can do to be our true self.

A Humble Theory of Our Evolution

You and I are evolving—all of us are. This evolution has been going on since the "beginning of time" and will continue into the infinite future. Typically we don't think about this too much.

I'm not the person I was when I was young. I'm not even the person I was five years ago, last year, or even last week. Yes, I'm older, but hopefully I am wiser. My personal evolutionary journey has been one of living through the various experiences of life with all their joy and all their pain, and learning from them. I suspect you feel the same way.

My personal journey began in the early 1950s in the deep South of the United States. I slowly became aware of the segregated culture I had been born into.

Like any child, I learned to navigate through my new world by looking outward, interacting with others, getting feedback, and then internalizing what had happened. I sought to maximize pleasure and minimize pain. I sought to fulfill personal needs such as nourishment, safety, and a sense of connectedness. To maintain our middle-class standard of living, both of my parents worked. I was kept secure and loved by an African-American nanny named Lolete. In my developing awareness, I imprinted upon her as my mother.

I remember that Lolete fed me, bathed me, and loved me. I have vague recollections of occasionally visiting her home and being aware that her personal environment was much different from the one in which I lived. Lolete traveled with my family on vacations to the beaches of Florida to take care of my brother and me. Besides my memories, the few old black-and-white photos in the family album are the only tangible items left from this relationship.

Before I turned five, my family moved to another city, leaving Lolete behind. This was normal in our culture, but not in my developing consciousness. I was heartbroken. My primary loving caretaker relationship had been snatched from my life. My parents did not understand my pain. My tears were met with punishment, so I learned to hide them. Through this outer experience, I internalized that something must be wrong with me. I buried deep within my unconsciousness the sense that I was not worthy as a human being to receive love.

This whole scenario and how I internalized it lay hidden from my awareness for decades, yet its effects played out time and time again in my life patterns. In moments of choice in my life when I wanted to do something, to be somebody, to move into a relationship with someone else, a quiet voice told me I was not worthy and led me to choices that reinforced that belief.

It's been my experience that many of us have moved through similar stories. We experienced some outer pain, inflicted upon us either intentionally or unintentionally. We internalized a personal story about the meaning of that pain, and then moved through life placing limits on ourselves based on those unacknowledged stories. Hopefully at some point, our life experiences allow us to bring into our awareness these past situations so that we can consciously make new choices going forward. That process is part of our personal development and growth, and is a major aspect of what I'm calling our *personal evolution*.

Growth and evolution come through many channels. Our education has developed us; our careers have developed us; our relationships have developed us. Much of our growth has come from these conscious arenas.

The point is this: We are born here on Earth, interact with the external world around us, and internalize what we have learned. All of this has contributed, either consciously or subconsciously, to who we are in this moment. This unfolding path of growth is my evolutionary story and yours.

If you're like I was, you probably haven't given much thought to the concept of evolution. It seems that you have more important things to do in your life. When you have considered the concept of evolution, you probably have seen it as a contentious scientific theory that divides religious people from scientific people. These two camps battle over the content of textbooks, and members of one camp display fish symbols on their cars in an attempt to sway public opinion in their direction.

Evolution's Current Debate

On one side of this debate is Darwinian evolutionary theory, which is accepted as fact in most scientific circles. The theory offers an explanation for how the physical life around us developed to its current state. We all know the basics—that there is an innate drive for life forms to survive and reproduce themselves. Central to the theory is the concept of "survival of the fittest": The expressions of physical life that are best suited for the environmental conditions in which they live are more likely to survive and produce more offspring carrying their traits. The ongoing dance between changing life conditions and the forms of life that developed to deal with those conditions is the story of evolution. This "dance" is how we reached our present state. Part of our personal heritage, as we will see, are the physical, mental, and emotional traits we express that served our ancestor's survival needs.

On the other side of the debate are those with a strong religious belief that leads to attachment to traditional stories presented in the Bible. If the Bible is taken literally (as many do), then it is impossible for Darwin's theory to be correct. According to the Bible, man's creation was driven by an external God's desire to create something special: humans formed in its own image, not shaped by evolutionary forces. Darwinian evolution is in direct opposition to a literal reading of the Genesis story. The Bible paints a human history that encompasses only thousands of years, a much shorter timeline than evolutionary forces would have required to bring about humanity. The dating of fossils and the evolutionary process both show that life has been developing through lengths of time extending into the millions of years; a fact that is clearly unacceptable to those who believe in the Bible's literal timeline.

Yet, evolution doesn't have to be an "either–or" debate. In my opinion, Darwinian evolution has been well established and proven correct. However, that doesn't mean we should discard the Bible and the wisdom that can be gleaned from it. It simply means we need to transcend a literal interpretation of the book and include its deeper meanings within a greater framework that incorporates Darwin's ideas.

In recent years, a growing number of people have begun to recognize that evolution is more than a physical process. In the past 20 or 30 years, there has been a growing expansion of the use of evolutionary principles in scientific disciplines other than biology. Scientists have had great success in explaining the development of societies, economies, psychological influences, and more by employing the idea of evolution. Evolutionary principles are serving to bring greater awareness of our spiritual development as well. It is beyond the scope of this book to review the impact of Darwin's theory in all these areas, but I suggest that the interested reader investigate some of the resources listed in the back of this book.

The point is this: Evolution is a fact. Yet, as I have described through my story of Lolete, the evolution I am speaking of is not limited to the mechanistic aspects of Darwin's theory. Rather, we see the truth in his theory as to how we got here physically, recognizing that our physical nature and those material forces are still at play in our lives. Yet, evolution also is occurring in the realm of the nonphysical, in our inner world—our consciousness. We will weave around this theme throughout the rest of the book.

Painting a Different Picture

At this point, I simply want to paint a picture in your mind about how this evolutionary path may be unfolding in your consciousness. First we must consider, what is *consciousness*? I am defining it here as a nonmaterial aspect that is available to us in two ways.

The first (and most familiar) aspect of consciousness is the conscious sense of awareness we all have, which is apparent in our thoughts and available memories. It's that sense within us that we think of as "me" when someone asks who we are. If I ask you to stop and look around the room, it is the aspect of you that read those words, decided to stop and look around the room (or not), and then thought about what you were reading or seeing. It is the part of you that witnesses and participates in your life experiences with a sense that you are aware of it all.

The second way that consciousness is available to us

is through subconscious thoughts and memories. Like my long-hidden memories of leaving my nanny, they dwell behind the scenes and impact our conscious thoughts and beliefs, frequently without our recognizing it. This second aspect of consciousness includes the part of your awareness that operates your bodily functions without you having to be cognizant of them. It takes in sensory experiences and determines if you need to be aware of them. Most of the input our senses receive in any given moment is not brought into our conscious awareness, but on some level we are aware of it.

The combination of our conscious thoughts and memories and our subconscious thoughts and beliefs is what I am calling "consciousness." I recognize that you may have a different definition. That's fine; simply keep my definition in mind when you read it here.

What I am offering here is the idea that our current evolution is about the developmental growth of our conscious and subconscious beliefs and patterns. To help you visualize this, I will describe in the next few paragraphs a sequence of images that may assist you in understanding the overall evolutionary path that I believe we are on. You don't have to believe it, but I am asking you to play along even if you think you aren't good at creating visualizations.

A Visualization

First, imagine in your mind's eye a vast ocean with lots of little waves rising up, peaking, and cresting above the ocean's surface. The waves rise and fall. Imagine this rising and falling in slow motion. Imagine pressing the pause button during this process so that you have a still picture of one moment in time, with all the waves that are cresting at that particular moment. Hold that image in your mind. It should look like a vast number of little peaks cresting upward from an infinite ocean.

Now, imagine that each of these waves is a human being. Imagine that each wave can direct its attention outwardly (above the surface of the ocean) or inwardly (below the surface). When a wave's attention is focused above the surface, it sees each wave as separate and apart from itself. It notices their differences; it senses their competition. When a wave's attention is focused below the surface, it sees each wave as rising from the same source. At this level, there are no differences and no need for competition. Just like these imaginary waves, we humans have the same choice: to look outward at our differences or inward to our common nature.

Now, staying with this visual image, I want you to visualize a sequence of how each wave (or human) is moving through a set of different approaches in how their attention is focused.

In the first phase, the wave's attention is focused outward, above the surface. It notices all the different waves and their interactions with each other. It notices how the waves are interacting with other things in the outer world. In trying to understand all these external interactions, this outward-looking wave may attempt to define numerous unseen powers that seem like gods controlling the buffeting of the waves. The wave sees itself as a victim to the whims of these external forces. The wave is in competition with the other waves. It's only ability to control life as a wave is to try to appease these external forces and hope for the best.

In the second phase, the wave's attention is still focused outward. However, now, in its attempt to understand all the external interactions, it has coalesced its story about external forces down to one, all-powerful God. The wave is still victim to this external force, and it is still in competition with the other waves. It still has no control, but at least now there's only one God to deal with. *If I can get on God's good side,* hopes the wave, *maybe he can help me in my competition with the other waves.*

In the third phase, the wave's attention continues to be focused outwardly. However, with its growing wisdom, the wave begins to see and better understand how the various external forces play out as they knock into one another. It measures what it sees and begins predicting with great success what will happen next. The wave starts to think that maybe there is no God out there, and thinks, *Maybe it's really about learning more of how these external forces work, and making better predictions so that I can control life.* The wave is still a victim to these external forces, but is becoming empowered by moving into a better understanding of how to use the forces. Life begins to be more about using this knowledge for self-benefit in competition with the other waves.

In the fourth phase, the wave's attention begins to turn downward, to under the surface. The wave recognizes that there are limits to its understanding of the above-the-surface world. There are things the wave can't seem to explain simply by measuring what's going on "out there." The wave begins to realize that even its attention and awareness come from someplace else. The wave recognizes that no matter how successful it is in its competition with the other waves, something is missing. At some point, the wave shifts its focus inward. This change brings new information. Yet, the wave is still mesmerized by the external life. It shifts its focus up and down (above the surface and below) and back and forth, attempting to understand what's really real and what's really important. The below-surface sense of connectedness begins to lessen the outer sense of competition.

In the fifth phase, the wave is at peace, moving its attention effortlessly both above and below the surface. It recognizes the value of the outer experiences but is no longer victim to them. Rather, the wave sees its below-surface nature as its real truth and draws strength from it. It recognizes that it is connected to all the other waves at its source. It recognizes that the interactions of the waves on the outer level are simply opportunities to gain experience and wisdom via that temporary path of a sense of separation. The wave begins to realize that the affinity, the love, it felt for other waves was simply a force that was moving its attention away from their differences and more inwardly, toward their similarities. The wave begins to realize that the entire process was set up for its growth and understanding, and comprehends that the ocean has embedded within the wave a special purpose or reason for existing. The wave begins to live that purpose, realizing that its purpose is designed not only to serve the wave individually, but also to serve all the other waves and the ocean itself.

These phases of the wave's movement through its awareness or consciousness are representative of our ultimate story. Each of us was born from the same source, and in that source we are united. Each of us rises out of that source and peers outward to our interactions with others, forgetting our commonality. Our focus is on our differences. Our meaning and understanding comes by trying to understand this outer aspect of life. Our stories about life "out there" and what it means evolve over time and experience. Finally, we return home and remember our truth. As we return home, we are wiser and see our home differently. We had to leave our source, to separate from it so we could return and know our home and unity from a different level.

This story has been expressed in many human tales over the years. It is the story of the prodigal son in the Bible. The hero's journey that mythologist Joseph Campbell wrote about also chronicles this path of growth. Each of us is moving through the story individually, and humanity is collectively moving through the story.

Stop and think about your life for a moment. You were born; you went through experiences leading you up to this moment. You are not the same person you were years ago. You have grown; you have evolved. Your consciousness (the combination of your conscious thoughts and memories and subconscious thoughts and beliefs) has changed over time. What has been your path? Where are you going?

Stop and think about humanity for a moment. Collectively, we came into being and have gone through historical experiences leading up to this moment. We are not the same people we were years ago. We have grown; we have evolved. Our consciousness (the combination of our conscious thoughts and memories and subconscious thoughts and beliefs) has changed over time. What has been our path? Where are we going?

This humble theory of evolution is simply this: We all came from the same source. To better understand the starting place, we had to forget where we came from and journey out into the world of form, where we experienced ourselves as separate and apart from one another. We moved through a path of trying to understand how this outer world works. Ultimately, our experiences are moving us back to our starting place—our source, our unity. When we return, we will know it at a much deeper level than if we had never taken the trip.

As stated in the words of acclaimed poet T.S. Eliot in his poem, *Little Gedding*:

> *We shall not cease from exploration*
> *And the end of all our exploring*
> *Will be to arrive where we started*
> *And know the place for the first time.*

The Challenge

Hopefully at this point, you are at least considering an expanded definition of the concept of evolution and how you and I, along with everyone else, are moving along a developmental path. The more you look at life through this kind of lens, the more you recognize that humanity is at a major crossroads. Most people who are paying attention sense this.

What are some of the symptoms that indicate that we are at such a moment?

I admit that the symptoms I see are based purely on my own personal observations and the feelings and judgments I have about what I observe. I offer them for your consideration; you may or may not agree. Basically, I feel frustration over the rising divisiveness occurring between humans. How is this showing up?

One of the major symptoms I see is a growing number of people who believe that their beliefs and values are better than everyone else's and there is no room for compromise. They believe they are right and other people are wrong, and that if everyone thought like they do, then the world would be a better place. They are so locked into seeing the world based on their own personal experience that there is no room for others to believe differently.

The fact is that people have had different life experiences and built different mental constructs of the world, colored by their life's path. Unfortunately, we generally can't sense these inner influences. Although it certainly is natural to have discernment so we can see that one idea or belief is more valid than another—for us—we are vulnerable to crossing into the world of our shadow when we seek to make others believe as we do. This occurs when we sense there is a battle of right and wrong occurring in our minds versus the minds of others—when we feel it is important that we "win" the battle of ideas while the other person "loses."

Discussion and debate are healthy when we're not attached to winning. They become unhealthy when it becomes important for us to prove the other person wrong. In such cases, our words can turn vitriolic and violent. In my observation, such actions are increasing.

Also on the increase is the trend of people believing strongly that their way of seeing the world is the only valid way, and they are convinced that their personal ideas must "win out" in the marketplace of ideas. They seek to grow their base of supporters who believe as they do. Now, it is natural for us to band together with like-minded individuals to share ideas and gain political clout. But again, there is a subtle shift into the shadow when we sense that "our group" has to "win" at the expense of other groups "losing." Tolerance of groups that believe differently from us should be a higher aspiration for humanity than the belief that our group's ability to generate more converts than other groups is more primary.

Consider for a moment the shift in public discourse in the past 10 years or so. The media and political debate used to acknowledge areas of agreement while allowing the space for differences of opinion. Now, there appears to be greater focus upon the extreme differences around issues, with less acknowledgment of points of commonality. It's as if the media are recognizing that we have so many choices and so much information coming at us that they must create a controversy to gain our attention. Unfortunately, they do this by pitting supporters of the far-fringe differences

Part One: Our Current Evolutionary Crossroads

of an issue against each other, while ignoring those that hold the middle ground. They invite to their programs the most controversial speakers and then feed them questions designed to stir the pot.

Personally, I find it hard not to feel frustration when I'm watching the speakers trying to out-duel one another—attacking the other's position, interrupting the other speaker, talking over one another, and treating each other disrespectfully. It's as if they have been thrown in a cage for a few minutes to verbally spar. Frequently, the presentation is less a dialogue to inform us than it is a fight to entertain us. The one with the most sound bites, or that makes the better points, is the winner.

It seems like almost every aspect of our culture gets thrown into this battle for supremacy. The middle ground in our political discourse, that fertile area of give-and-take that led to higher political solutions, has all but disappeared in recent years. In some people's minds, *compromise* has become a dirty word. In some circles, seeking common ground is seen as a sign of weakness, failure, and losing.

There are religions whose focus has shifted from offering their teachings into a forceful proselytizing. Instead of allowing individuals to seek a faith that resonates with them, some religions pressure people into converting to their faith. Again, it's a subtle shift from an intent of offering ideas they believe in, to the actions of judging and attacking others for believing differently. All major faiths have some fundamentalist groups that have slipped into viewing their spirituality as a battle to be fought—one with winners and losers.

The system of science has not been immune to the shift from seeking the empirical truth into the battle for whose "truth" is right. In some cases, these battles pit scientist against scientist. In others, they turn scientists and religious leaders against one another. In still other cases, some scientists can be seen moving into a sort of scientific fundamentalism rather than keeping a healthy open mind, which is prerequisite for scientific discovery.

Consider how some aspects of science have been co-opted into the political arena for debate. The scientific reality of climate change continues to be debated. The well-proven theory of evolution continues to come under attack by religious fundamentalists. There has been an increase of the so-called "skeptics" that frequently move beyond the bounds of presenting pure science and into the realm of attacking those who don't believe as they do. At some point, every topic seems to get dragged down into a battle —with winners and losers.

Another symptom I witness of our growing human crisis is that people, in their attempt to gain a degree of safety and security through the accumulation of possessions, move into the place of seeing the never-ending growth of their personal wealth as the prime purpose of life. Again, to be clear, I'm not saying there's anything wrong with being prosperous. Creating abundance and wealth and enjoying a life of affluence certainly is one of the gifts of living life. There's nothing wrong with desiring a certain standard of living and a prosperous life—but again, a subtle shift occurs when we move to the place where gaining more wealth is seen as more important than anything else. We must win more "stuff," even if it's at your expense—that is, you lose.

The Wall Street greediness of recent years is a symptom of this psychological shift. The growing division in the distribution of wealth (between the small number of "haves" and the growing number of "have-nots") is another indication of our problem. Whenever a person bends the rules of ethics to successfully make more money, it becomes increasingly easier for others around them to bend the same rules. As it says in the Bible, "For the love of money is the root of all kinds of evil" (1 Timothy 6:10). This love has created an ethical crisis of great proportions.

Another symptom I witness is the growing attempt by a minority of people to control our social systems. These individuals are driven by either selfish greed or fervent ideology. Healthy debate leading to the creation of systems that work for everyone's highest benefit is a good thing. We need strong and effective governments that meet the needs of all. Religions that offer things like personal meaning and comfort in times of challenge are beneficial. Maintaining an educational system that assists each person in developing the tools and opportunities to live a healthy and successful life is something we should all support. Corporations that provide us useful products to make life better are desirable.

Yet again, there is plenty of evidence of attempts to co-opt our social systems by individuals and groups that seek to win at the expense of others. Motivated by greed, some of our financial institutions and corporations use their wealth to lobby Congress to maintain rules and regulations that benefit them at the expense of the rest of the country. They seek to limit the government's ability to oversee their business dealings or the safety of their products. They want to pay less in taxes than others, or obtain government subsidies to support their corporate activities. They want to win, even if others lose.

The desire to force a belief system on those that think differently has led to vicious political battles in recent years. Those whose religious beliefs cause them to abhor abortion seek to institutionalize eliminating its availability even for those who believe differently. Those whose religious beliefs deny the scientific validity of evolution attempt to force nonscientific options into our classrooms over the objections of those who believe differently. They perceive that forcing their beliefs on others—winning—is more important than allowing others the freedom to believe and act as they choose.

I could continue with more examples, but you probably get the point. No doubt you could create your own list of frustrating experiences where individuals have shifted into the place of materialistic greediness or ideologically driven righteousness, to the point that they have turned the world into a battle of winners and losers. My point here is not to dwell on the negative. Rather, my intent is twofold: One desire is for us to notice and acknowledge this growing gap between our highest vision of humanity and what we are experiencing in the world, and to recognize that this gap is reaching a critical point where we must act now to bridge it. My second hope is that by highlighting the experiences that are less than what we are capable of creating, through observing the contrast, we can create a vision of what we would like to experience instead.

So, what are our choices here?

In one direction lies a world of peace and prosperity, where all humans are valued and have the opportunity to express themselves and succeed. In this world, technology makes life easier, the Earth's resources are valued, and humanity serves as a good steward of the planet.

In the other direction lies a world of violence and scarcity, where humans are in competition for limited resources. Some of us will come out as winners; most will end up as losers with little opportunity. In this world, technology may assist us, but it might overtake us. The Earth is changed for the worse by humanity's neglect.

Although your descriptions may differ slightly, I have little doubt that most of you have looked to the future and seen similar choices ahead. Which road will we follow? How can we make the best choice? What can you do? What can I do?

The Bridge to Our Future

A few years ago, I was contemplating my concerns about the present state of humanity. It's easy to become pessimistic when we start thinking about all the challenges currently facing us. Yet, something within me sensed there had to be a way to move from the challenges of the present to a more hopeful, utopian-like future. When meditating on this idea, the metaphor of a bridge came to me.

The concept of a bridge represented a path across a schism. If our current circumstances, which are so much "in our face," seem so overwhelming, I couldn't help but visualize us humans running full-steam toward a cliff. We were like the cartoon character Wiley Coyote, chasing the roadrunner one moment and finding ourselves in midair the next. Tantalizingly, off in the distance was "the other side" representing safety, security, and prosperity. How do we move confidently into the future without falling off the cliff? How do we move to the oasis on the other side where we know things will work out for the best? Enter "the bridge."

It became apparent that we need to build a bridge from our current challenging circumstances to the future that is possible. The bridge would cross the gap between where we find ourselves now and where we desire to be in the future. The bridge was the way to overcome the seemingly impossible odds of current earthly problems.

As I played with this metaphor, I realized that both building and crossing the bridge would occur only as more people like you and I became *conscious*. Conscious of what? Conscious that we are evolving. Conscious that we are faced with enormous challenges. Conscious that there is the possibility of a better future than current circumstances would suggest. Conscious that we all play a role in moving us to the greater possibilities.

This awareness led me to my name my website *Conscious Bridge* a few years ago. My writings there have been based on increasing conscious awareness of our issues and our role in evolving, individually and collectively, to that enhanced future. I invite you to visit the site (www.consciousbridge.com) to find out more.

Although there are many things I believe you and I can do to advance humanity's prospects, I will condense them into three basic actions. These three charges, which I am asking you to consider making a part of your life's pattern, are detailed in the next three sections of this book.

First, I want us to consider reorienting our focus away from seeing how you, I, and everyone else are different, and shifting it into a focus on how we are alike. The key here is that whatever we focus our attention upon tends to grow. If we focus on our differences, then we tend to get more conflict. If we focus on the similarities, then we tend to get more cooperation. Hence, the next section of the book offers a number of ideas on how we are alike.

Second, I want us to consider maintaining a focus on a vision of what humanity's highest potential might be. Stephen Covey, in his book, *The 7 Habits of Highly Effective People*, encouraged us to begin with the end in mind. The Bible reminds us that where there is no vision, the people perish. Every project manager and business leader knows that the key to success is to outline where you want to go. We must have some degree of the collective vision we are working toward if we want to attain it. This doesn't mean we all must agree on every detail, but there is value in some degree of consensus around characteristics of the future we would like to experience. The third section of the book considers some options.

Third, and most importantly, I want you to *be yourself*. I want you to be the highest vision of who you can be in this lifetime. I want you to tap into your external life's patterns and inner callings to identify the special reason you are here living your life at this time. It is my sincere belief that you have a gift, a talent, some unique ability that you were given to use fully in this lifetime. Maybe you're using it, maybe not. I want you to identify it and begin to expand your experience of it. As you do, you will enjoy your life more, feel greater fulfillment, and your life will expand in all areas for the best. Acting in your own self-interest to be yourself in this way will also call you to give your gift to others. This self-action becomes an important plank in building our bridge to the future.

Part Two:

Focusing Upon Our Commonalities

In the second section of the book, we will explore the following ideas:

- If we stop and think about it, we can identify many ways that we are all the same.
- One major characteristic we share is the sense of our individual life moving through time.
- Another major characteristic we share is the sense that our individual life was dropped into a larger human timeline.
- We all share the desire to believe a certain story about the meaning of this larger human narrative.
- The differences in our "meaning stories" frequently cause us to focus upon our differences.
- We all share the dual experience of being both a physical animal and a nonphysical "higher" being.
- These dual experiences generate desires within us—desires that often are at odds with each other.
- We all have the ability to direct our lives through our conscious, free-will choices.

A Brief List of Human Common Characteristics

What we give our time and energy to is what tends to grow in our life. Withdrawing our time and energy from something causes it to diminish. We will explore this point in greater detail in a later chapter.

For now, I simply ask you to consider how you might shift your attention away from emphasizing our differences toward emphasizing our similarities. This shift must begin with setting an intention to do so. It must begin with your making the choice, within your thoughts, to more frequently notice how we are alike than how we are different.

I'm asking you to begin developing the habit of noticing ways in which you are like other people. This is especially important when you become emotional over the actions or comments of another person. If they push your buttons somehow, then build in some "mental brakes" that keep you from reacting. In that moment, cultivate a realization of how that person is similar to you. Recognize that if you had lived their life, you might be acting the way they are. Release your judgment and open your heart.

So, how are we all the same?

I encourage you to stop reading for a moment and create a list of ways you see humans as being alike. Create your list and then continue reading, comparing what you listed with my ideas below.

If we were to brainstorm a list of the ways that humans are similar, it might include some of these points:

- We all have the same basic physical structure.
- We all have the same physiological needs for water, air, and food.
- We all have the same need to eliminate bodily waste.
- We all have the desire for love and friendship.
- We all have a physiological need for sex.
- We all have the need for periodic sleep, including deep sleep where we dream.
- We all had parents.
- We all have inherited tendencies from our parents.
- We all have DNA.
- We all have a desire for comfort, to maximize pleasure and minimize pain.
- We all have a desire to be viewed as competent.
- We all want to be seen as physically attractive.
- We all want the best for our children and grandchildren.
- We all want to have a level of wealth that provides for our needs.
- We all want new and entertaining experiences.
- We all want to be healthy and physically fit.
- We all want to eat tasty food.
- We all tend to identify ourselves with a group or groups, be it through ethnicity, nationality, religion, occupation, or some other common denominator.
- We all have a desire to understand how life works and its greater meaning.

I could go on and on with this list. You probably have some ideas that came to mind that I didn't include.

My point is this: You, I, and everyone on the planet share a great deal. We are very much alike. Our physical nature, our desires, and our emotional needs are identical at their base level.

Behind all of this, I would like us to reflect on one more way in which we are identical: We all share a common story.

Born into the Human Story

Our Personal Timeline

See if you can relate to this: I walk through life with a sense of personal history trailing me. There are facts I can relate to others, such as my place and date of birth, my parents' names, where I have lived, and where I went to school. Then, there are the details of my jobs, relationships, children, and grandchildren. This is the data I use to complete forms.

Beyond all these facts are my memories. I don't remember the moment of my birth, but I have a lot of memories regarding the story of my birth. I remember my mother telling me that after my older brother was born, she and my dad decided to have another child. As I recall the tale, she became pregnant once, maybe twice, and lost the baby. When she became pregnant with me, she had to be very careful not to lose the baby again. She wanted me so much that she had to stay in bed during the last phase of the pregnancy. Obviously, she gave birth to me just fine. Although I don't remember any of this directly, I've heard the stories so many times that they have become part of the fabric of who I am. You probably have similar family stories regarding your conception and birth.

Next come the early memories, a jumbled collection of brief snippets of visual images from my early years. Crawling on the floor of our first house, avoiding the floor furnace, hiding in the bushes outside, picking mint beside the house, my dad riding me around on a bicycle—things like that. Here is where I have the memories of Lolete that

I discussed previously. Most people tell me that, similarly, they can only recall a handful of memories from their first few years.

As I grow older (that is, as I mentally move forward through my history), I have more detailed memories. At some point, there is a leveling off where I have the sense of more total recollection from that point forward, even though I don't truly remember most of the occurrences of my life. Some days I can barely remember a few days back!

The point here is this: The sum total of who I am contains this historical record of things I had been told about my early life, as well as my later direct, personal memories. These memories are combined with various "facts" I have absorbed from my culture, education, media bombardment, relationships, and so on. All of this melds into a sense of being this person (me) who has moved along through time. I drag my history around with me, adding to it daily. Each moment of every day, I am forging ahead into the future. Yes, I live in "the now," but it sure goes by fast!

Do you relate to my life story? Of course, your details are different, but the general sense of experiencing your life as a timeline of your past history moving into the future is what I'm asking about. We all have this sense of personal history feeding our story of who we are and impacting our thoughts and aspirations for the future. Everyone you meet has the same experience; it's only the details that differ.

Our Common Timeline

Just as I have a timeline and you have a timeline (the story we tell ourselves about our past leading up to the present and having an impact on our future), humanity has a collective timeline. We have a story we tell ourselves about how humanity got here, the purpose of our existence, and how this relates to the way we live our lives. Yes, there are variations on the details of what we believe is true about our collective story, but consider again that everyone you meet has the same sense of a larger human narrative.

Another common denominator in our collective story is that humanity's story was underway when we as an individual arrived on the scene, and it continues when we leave. It's as if there's been a long movie playing, which was already in progress when we got here. We come in, try to pick up on what's going on, interact with the other actors, and bow out at the end of our life. It is this sense of our individual lives in the context of our larger collective lives that mystic Joel Goldsmith described as our lives being like a "parentheses in eternity."

In addition, the larger story seems so "big" compared to our small stories' "smallness" that we often feel powerless to change humanity's direction. Who are we in our little actions to impact the vastness of the world and its great momentum? Often, the best we think we can do to effect positive change is to live our lives in a decent way and hope that we made things a little better for the people close to us. Unfortunately, many feel so helpless to change the big picture that they don't even try, and they spend their lives focused primarily on selfish needs. Perhaps if we knew that our lives made a difference, we would be less inclined to live them in such an egocentric way.

Yet while we are here, our understanding of (and beliefs about) the "big story" guides our thoughts and actions in the "little story" of our individual life. Each of us adopts an interpretation of this "back story" of humanity's existence that drives how we see life and determines our choices.

Some of this is conscious; much is subconscious, but it's all part of what I am describing as *consciousness*.

Our Different "Back Stories"

So what are these "back stories" about the reason we're all here? Although there probably are as many different stories as there are people, there are enough common factors in the way people view life that we can lump the ideas together into just a few stories.

Developmental social scientists have noticed these commonalities, and their data has led them to create categorizations of levels of human growth. These rankings, or developmental stages, relate to what I am calling our different stories. We might also refer to these stories as our *worldviews*. Various theorists have created their own names for the different worldviews, and they have suggested varying numbers of developmental levels as well. For more information on these ideas, refer to the Resources section of this book.

I'm calling them "back stories" to connect them in your awareness to a method actors use to "get into character": They create a fictitious history for the person they are pretending to be. This back story won't show up in the finished movie or play, but is something the actors feel into to help them understand their character's motivation for the present-day action. The story never happened except in the actor's imagination, but the actor knows that by embodying this made-up history, he will make choices that will be much more realistic and consistent.

Similarly, we have bought into a back story for our lives. We may tell ourselves it is real, but is it? Much of it has simply been "given to us" by our culture, education, family, and so forth. For much of what we have accepted as true, we may not have had any direct personal experience to lead us to that "truth." Yet, we have acted on these stories as if they were real.

For right now, I simply want to offer three different back stories that are prevalent in our modern world. There are other common stories that many humans hold, especially in developing countries, but I am presenting these three because it's likely you will recognize them. I'll call these stories *traditional, material,* and *humanistic,* though you may know them by other names, such as *pre-modern, modern,* and *postmodern.* The third story, when associated with the group of people that embody that idea, is sometimes called "cultural creatives," a term coined by sociologist Paul H. Ray and psychologist Sherry Ruth Anderson in their book by that name.

We'll look at each of these worldviews individually. First, let's consider the *traditional* back story.

The word *traditional* contains the word *tradition,* which says a lot about this viewpoint. Those who look at life in this way place great importance upon truths, rituals, beliefs, and ways of living that have been handed down from the past. Honoring the past is seen as being of the utmost importance. Growing and changing with the current times is not encouraged. Hence, there is a high degree of conservative behavior, both in religion and politics, exhibited by those who hold this story.

A person with the typical traditional outlook has received their back story on life's big picture from their parents and culture, and they've accepted it as a truth not to be questioned. Of major importance in this story are the details disseminated by the individual's religious upbringing.

For example, using Christianity, the major religion in the

United States, salient details of the Christian story say that an external God (generally pictured as an old man) spoke to certain people 2000 to 3000 years ago, and these people recorded God's word in the Bible. Included in that book is a description of our creation: God created Adam and Eve, and everyone else is a descendent of those two, with the Earth and its creation occurring no more than 10,000 years ago, which was the beginning of humanity's timeline.

The Christian story also provides us direction as to why we are here. The traditional story says, essentially, that we are here to gain "salvation." Because Adam and Eve ate the forbidden fruit in the Garden of Eden, we all have been condemned to be born on Earth as "sinners." According to a number of the Protestant sects of Christianity, our only hope lies in our attempts to become "saved" by accepting that the person of Jesus is our savior. This acceptance gives meaning to our life on Earth and provides us an eternal life in the hereafter.

If you are Christian and maintain a traditional view of life, this story guides many of your life choices. Neither the Bible nor the story is to be questioned; upholding their power is of the utmost importance. One's religion, its teachings, and its rituals are not to be altered, since their original dissemination to humanity was from this external God himself.

This example is a brief description of the story of Christianity, which is one of many faiths that place importance on handing down their traditions from generation to generation. This traditional viewpoint is prevalent among many Jewish, Muslim, and other religious groups. However, I would hasten to point out that simply because a person is a follower of a certain faith, it does not necessarily mean they view life from a traditional viewpoint. There are many religious people who hold other worldviews.

Another key point is that, although it can be easy to view certain conflicts as being between one religion and another (for example, between the Jewish and Moslem faiths in the Middle East), it is not simply a matter of one religion versus another. Rather, the conflicts are really between one traditional worldview group that happens to believe in one religion and another traditional worldview group that happens to believe in another religion. Both groups are locked into not questioning the stories they've been given, and their tight adherence to these stories is a central aspect of their conflict.

Another interesting aspect of these traditional stories (one that helps keep them embedded in their culture) is that life's rewards are deferred to life beyond the physical realm—the afterlife. The attitude is, "I believe that my suffering while I am here on earth is justified by the gifts I'll be given when I leave here. The efforts of others to sway me from my faith, by either material possessions or rational arguments, are seen as temptations to deter me from my path. I must deny the temptations and stay focused on my heavenly rewards."

In fact, many people that hold a traditional viewpoint see "evil" as a thing unto itself, which generally is personified in the form of an external being (the Devil or Satan) who plays out an external battle with God or his disciples in a good versus evil tug-of-war for our souls. Any attempt to convince people that their traditional worldview is somehow in error can be viewed as the workings of this evil force.

Just as salvation, heaven, and eternal life exist as a divine intent for the individual, this divine intent guides society as well. Hence, political issues are closely tied to religious issues, as in the belief that "my actions in the political arena should be in alignment with God's will for our collective lives." Those holding a traditional viewpoint believe that maintaining the sanctity of marriage between a man and a woman and bringing religious teachings into the schools are important political issues.

This traditional viewpoint carries over into other areas of society as well. If there have always been the rich and the poor, that is a differentiation among classes, and that class structure should continue. Seeking to use the government and social systems to equalize educational opportunities and material wealth among people is counter to the tradition of allowing a person to "lift themselves up by their own bootstraps" to gain success. The history of one's country and the intentions of the founders are important factors in this worldview. Those holding the traditional viewpoint feel they must maintain that sense of unchanging continuity. For example, in the United States there are individuals that frequently cite the actions of the country's founding fathers, believing that what was successful in the creation of our country in the 1700s is critical for our success now, over 200 years later.

In traditional groups there is a great deal of nostalgia for the past, a longing for "the good old days." This includes such things as for a desire for "the simple life" when people lived on farms, there were clearly differentiated roles between men and women, romantic relationships were only between men and women, authority was not questioned, and so on. There truly is a desire to "freeze the clock" so we don't progress any further into a changing future. If they could, many traditionalists would reverse the clock to some mythical point in the past when things were better than they are now.

Are you starting to have a sense of this back story? Can you think of people you know personally, or are aware of in the media, that look at life this way? A large number of people in modern culture hold this worldview. You may be one.

Second, let's consider the *material* back story.

As the name implies, people that hold this story see physical matter—that is, *material*—as primary. This viewpoint has its roots in the origin of science. Those that first employed empirical measurements as a means of determining how the universe works often were branded as heretics by the church when their findings were in conflict with religious dogma. To circumvent this persecution, René Descartes proposed that the physical realm of matter and energy belonged to the study of science, while the nonmaterial realm of the mind and soul belonged to religion.

As science grew in its ability to explain the workings of the physical world, it brought a higher standard of living, along with tremendous technological advances. This success brought with it the sense that science can meet all our needs. To a degree, science became the new religion. It also passed along its story about the creation of the world and the purpose of our lives, a story that many of us learned in school.

The science story of our creation goes only as far back as the "Big Bang," about 14 billion years ago. Science offers no explanation as to what existed before this great "singularity," nor does it attempt to offer meaning as to why it occurred or why we exist. Science does offer many details regarding how we got from the Big Bang to where we are now (a story we will review later). Suffice to say this story is the backdrop of the timeline on which we have been placed for our life experiences, if you hold this worldview.

If you look at life from a material worldview, all of life is like a bunch of widgets, both large and small. Looking downward, we see the entire universe as being comprised of smaller and smaller material pieces—molecules, atoms, electrons and neutrons, quarks, and so on. These physical items are the "building blocks" of greater and greater physical structures. Looking upward to the heavens, we see a material universe comprised of planets, stars, and galaxies in tremendous numbers.

In the material system, success in understanding life comes through understanding how all of these widgets work together in relation to the known forces such as gravity, electromagnetism, and the strong and weak nuclear forces that act upon them. The more we determine how things work, the more we have the power to control them. Hence, the meaning of life is to control the physical universe for our own gain.

All of life now is comprised of things that we try to measure, control, and possess. At an early age, we grasp the importance of learning specific external "facts" that we repeat on tests to be rewarded with material "grades." We go on to college to get a "degree" so that hopefully we will get a better "job" where we will make more "money" so that we can have a bigger "house" and finer material possessions. Add to that "material possession" list belongings that we might not necessarily view as "things," such as acquiring a spouse, children, and friends. Even experiences like world travel and vacations, fine dining, and the like all become "things" that we have "done." Life becomes a game where the goal is to gain more and more stuff in all its forms.

People with the material worldview see themselves

competing with other people for power and possessions. The purpose of life is to strive and achieve—to win even at the expense of others. We've all heard the cliché, "He who dies with the most stuff wins." Many people believe that.

Faith, God, and religion frequently are seen as archaic myths from the past. However, in some cases, we see people professing to believe in a religion in order to attain a material goal. Success in some circles (especially politics) can come only if one is the member of the "right religion." Hence, association with a religion becomes less spiritually motivated and more like other "club memberships" that can be put on a list and used for outer gain.

Truly being concerned about understanding any inner world is seen as immaterial to meeting the needs of external life. Taken to its extreme in this worldview, our inner consciousness is seen as merely a byproduct of the firing of our brain's physical neurons. *Mind* equals *brain*, pure and simple. The underlying belief is in the power of material science to solve our needs. It has done a good job of convincing us that there is nothing it can't do.

For those who hold this worldview, anything contrary to the scientific viewpoint is seen as non-rational thinking, to be equated with being small-minded. The mentally weak, it is believed, tend to see things where they don't exist—to believe in myths simply because they bring some comfort in life. Pity the person who believes in religion or spirituality, the paranormal, or any experience that cannot be explained by material science! And, if the person offers any scientific evidence that seems to point to a non-material realm, it is seen as invalid because in the material realm, it simply can't be.

The material worldview has given us many gifts including modern medicine, which has raised our standard of living and lengthened our lives. The material mindset looks to the future and sees a world where we continue to expand our bodily limits by use of drugs and artificial body parts. The material worldview says our goal is to live longer and longer. In this game, maybe the real winner is the one with the most stuff who never dies!

A material worldview places great importance on technology, corporations, Wall Street, and faith in an ever-continuing economic growth. This is another area in which certain advancements clearly have improved our lives. But someone locked into the material worldview believes that we must continue making better and better things, which we sell more and more of, so as to have higher and higher profits forever and ever. Feeding the economic, material engine is crucial to life, regardless of the costs to society and the Earth.

Are you starting to get a sense of this back story? Can you think of people you know personally, or are aware of in the media, that look at life this way? A large number of people in modern culture hold this worldview. You may be one.

Finally, let's consider the third predominant story in modern culture: the *humanistic* back story.

As you might imagine, this worldview values our "humanness" as primary. What does that mean?

First, it means that all people, and their needs and opinions, must be considered when making decisions for the collective. Every person is important. In this system, I must canvass everyone to become aware of their desires and seek solutions that meet the needs of as many people as possible. Taking this idea to its fullest expression, I must seek solutions that involve everyone and are determined by consensus.

Second, it means that my purpose in life is to fully explore my life and its relationship to everyone else. I am called to transcend traditional religions as well as material possessions so as to look inside myself and meet needs that have an inner source. Exploring life to the fullest, "tasting" experiences, and incorporating them into my personally determined meaning of existence is essential to my reason for being. My psychological and personal development is critical.

In this system, there is a part of me that recognizes the limitations of both religion and science. Instead of following a specific, traditional religious path, I seek to taste many paths and create my own way to experience God. Although I value the benefits of science and technology, I realize that material wealth does not bring happiness.

All religious and spiritual paths, both the traditional and the very non-traditional, are open for me to pursue. I can pick and choose the pieces I like from them, to craft my own spiritual developmental path. This is the "new age" where I am able to tap ancient and modern truths and forge new meanings from my personal synthesis of them. My happiness, and the happiness of others, is part of the meaning of life.

Yet, I still feel there is a larger story or longer timeline I've been dropped into. For the most part, aspects of the Big Bang back story make sense to me, but I also see its limitations. Life can't be all just widgets bouncing around, randomly affected by physical forces. There must be meaning behind it all. Perhaps there is an intent and direction behind evolution, and not necessarily the old religious story—for why else would humans and our advanced consciousness exist?

With the humanistic worldview, there exists within me

a dichotomy between personal growth and the recognition that I am tied to everyone else and the entire world. Hence, I have a great interest in the environment, as well as in the rights of others. My relationship with the world, and with other people, is key. I volunteer for environmental causes, give money to social causes, and promote equality among all humans. Ultimately, I know that my specialness as a human (and yours too) is about becoming all I can be—becoming a *self-actualized* person.

Interestingly, this worldview was held by only a tiny speck of humanity until the last half of the twentieth century, when it blossomed. Now, it is estimated that approximately 25 percent or more of Americans are these "cultural creatives."

Are you starting to get a sense of this back story? Can you think of people you know personally, or are aware of in the media, that look at life this way? A large number of people in modern culture hold this worldview. You may be one.

These three worldviews are primary within modern Western culture. I have attempted to simplify them here for ease in painting a mental picture for you. However, real life never fits into neat, tidy boxes. Many people have aspects of more than one of these worldviews at play in their lives. Often, different worldviews are used in a sort of compartmentalized way in different areas of our life. For example, one might be somewhat traditional in their religious life, while being materialistic in their careers. It's not uncommon for people to switch between these viewpoints based on the needs of the moment.

However, generally speaking, one of three these ways of looking at life tends to be predominant in most people. We often forget that we ourselves possess a worldview that guides how we look at life. When we bump into other people who think differently, we tend to judge them negatively for their beliefs. It often escapes our awareness that our miscommunications with one another person frequently are due to our different stories. The first step in healing those differences is being aware of the different worldviews and how each has served an evolutionary purpose.

All of these worldviews are a part of our consciousness. As I described them, you probably identified one as being closest to what you believe. However, as you go through your day-to-day life making choices based on these beliefs, it's likely that your dominant worldview is not in your conscious awareness. For most of us, our worldviews lie within the "para-conscious" aspect of our awareness. (*Para-conscious* is the field of awareness just beyond the typical conscious state, where greater levels of information and abilities are available to us.) Our worldview was forged as the best understanding of our larger human story based upon our personal experiences and the surrounding culture. In other words, our personal life conditions allow our worldview to emerge as the best evolutionary way of seeing and understanding the world around us.

We tend to think there's only one true reality "out there." The truth is there are multiple realities. There is a complex dance between our consciousness and our outer life experiences. Our outer experiences provide the conditions that our consciousness evolves to handle in the optimum way. The "fittest people" are those whose consciousness has best evolved to survive in the world they live in. Cultural creatives would not have lasted long back in humanity's early history, when physical survival was tougher.

Yet, even as our worldview evolved to best meet our life conditions, it always was present in our para-conscious, guiding our thoughts and beliefs. It became so invisible to us that we tended to forget it was there, as it silently led us into believing that the reality it presents to us is the only reality there is.

The problem is that life is not static—our conditions can change. If we "grow with the times," our worldview will shift to be the one most advantageous for the new conditions. Our growth feeds our success; we become "fitter" for our new world. If we don't grow, we feel out of step with the world around us.

The complexity of modern life can lead to world conditions that vary within the same culture. We see this in current Western life. Some conditions have led large groups of people to see life through a traditional lens, while other conditions have allowed the materialist viewpoint or humanistic worldview to be more appropriate. What are the different factors that lead to different conditions and varying viewpoints in such close geographical proximity? These can be the differences in the areas of the country, growing up in different neighborhoods, living in different socioeconomic conditions, being exposed to different religions or spiritual beliefs, the nature of the education we receive, and more. Consider the example that the worldview of a child who grows up in a fundamentalist Christian family and is home-schooled is more likely to have a traditional outlook than a child who grows up in a family that pushed her to compete with others to be accepted at Harvard University and to make as much money as she can on Wall Street or in corporate settings.

Ultimately, we end up interacting with a range of people that view life differently from us. The result is that we can't agree on what is "real," or even on what is important. They judge us, wondering how we could think like we do. We judge them, wondering how could they think like they do. Whose reality is right? We believe ours is right, regardless of what it is.

The truth is that each of us defines our reality in our own minds. Instrumental in defining our reality is the "invisible" worldview that we have adopted as truth. That worldview then quietly guides our conscious thoughts in a particular direction, reinforcing our personal sense of what is real.

The key to shifting our focus away from differences and toward commonalities is to recognize that we all have these silent worldviews within us. You do; I do; everyone we meet does. The more we disagree on the basic issues of life, the more likely that the culprit is this generally undetectable belief structure. Bringing worldviews into our awareness allows us a greater chance to bridge our differences.

The next time you find yourself in an argument with someone and just can't see how they believe what they believe, stop and remind yourself that both of you share the experience of having a personal timeline that has entered into humanity's larger timeline. Both of you have created stories about the meaning of life, and these stories are the foundation of your beliefs. On the surface, you may be arguing over details based on different experiences. At your core, the structure of your life patterns is the same. Focus on your core similarities, and agree to disagree on the surface details.

Living in Two Worlds

Recently my wife and I attended a spiritual conference led by an extremely dynamic speaker. This woman ran around the room interacting with the audience, giving us information, answering questions, and leading us through experiential processes. She certainly was, on some level, "in the zone" as she imparted knowledge and flowed with the needs of the group. I was taking notes and learning.

Eventually, my internal desire to gain this wisdom and meet my mental and spiritual needs was being overridden by basic bodily needs: I had to go to the bathroom! I could see that I wasn't alone in this situation, as I watched person after person slink in and out of the room to attend to their physical needs. Eventually the speaker realized that the consciousness in the room had shifted, and she called a break.

This situation calls attention to something that may seem obvious: We all live in two worlds. Clearly, we live in a material world. We have physical bodies and processes related to a physical evolutionary past. These bodies have material needs for food, water, safety, and the ability to reproduce.

No matter what our higher motivations may be in a particular moment, thirst, hunger, or illness will knock our lofty ambitions out of our awareness. In those moments, we truly remember that we are physical animals.

Our senses and attention are drawn each day to this outer world. We navigate around physical stuff—our house, car, possessions, money, and so on. Most of our life seems focused on interactions with physical things and physical people via our relationships.

Yet, we also live in another world—one that clearly is not physical but is our "interior." It is the world of our consciousness, thoughts, and spiritual nature. Our internal understanding of each other lies in this dimension. It is the *metaphysical* arena (which means "beyond the physical").

We hang out in this world in our minds all the time, even if we believe the inner world doesn't truly exist. This is where we experience what William James called the "stream of consciousness": that floating river of thoughts that continuously passes by our awareness[1]. Meditators who have tried to stop this flow frequently call it the "monkey mind" in recognition of how it leaps magically from thought to thought, like a monkey jumping from branch to branch, in spite of our best efforts to stop it.

Individuals whose worldview is locked firmly in a materialistic, scientific way of perceiving deny that this interior world really exists. They say it is an "epiphenomenon" of the firing of the neurons in our brain—that is, our consciousness is simply a byproduct of these material processes. In their view, we have deluded ourselves into believing that it has some deep meaning and importance when the only meaning it may have is that it provided some evolutionary advantage in the past. Hence, those who accidentally gave rise to this illusory sense of self had a better chance of living longer and passing along the illusory byproduct to their children. The irony, of course, is that these "scientists" use their personal experience of this "byproduct" to label it thusly!

In the materialist worldview, our attempts to view this inner awareness and see it as real or having deep meaning is viewed as the delusional thinking of an ignorant person. Religion is seen as an organizational relic of the mythic beliefs of yesteryear. In this view, the spiritual experiences of any humans (whether they came from the past and drove the creation and growth of our religions or came from the present and the experiences of the "spiritual but not religious" crowd) obviously must be the product of strange internal wirings of our brains that served a past evolutionary need. Everything has a material explanation—if we cannot find one, then it simply is not "real." Therefore, psychic experiences, from premonitions to mind-over-matter to remote viewing and more, cannot exist in the materialist viewpoint—in spite of the overwhelming scientific evidence that proves their validity.

We all acknowledge the importance of science and reason as ways of "knowing." Yet, we also need to acknowledge that there are inner ways of knowing as well—namely, intuition and sources for which we have no label.

The point here is not to say that one way is correct and the other is not—that one way of being is real and the other is not. That's the old philosophical argument of idealism versus materialism. We need to let go of that "either-or" kind of thinking and move to a place where we recognize that both ideas are valid: We live in a world with an animal past and physical nature driven by our DNA and physical needs, and we also live in a world where we are called to higher levels of being in nonphysical realities.

The truth is that we live in two worlds simultaneously, and we need to keep that fact at the forefront of our awareness. It is one more way in which humans are alike.

Let's look at a couple of ways that our outer nature and our inner nature intersect—the evolutionary structure of our brains and the hardwiring within us of certain desires—and how this physical self can be at odds with our highest intentions.

The Triune Brain

In the 1960s, neuroscientist Paul MacLean put forth the theory that the human brain consisted of three basic parts, each evolving sequentially in our evolutionary past. Our "triune brain" consists of the reptilian complex, the limbic system, and the neocortex[2]. Carl Sagan later popularized this theory with this book, *The Dragons of Eden*, although he believed that what we considered our "minds" were simply our brains created through evolutionary forces[3]. Although recent evidence appears to discount a purely evolutionary path moving from the development of one part of the brain to the next (and also calls into question the pure distinctions in the descriptions of the roles of each "brain" first suggested), the model remains popular as a means of describing how our brain functions through three broad clusters, each with their own purpose. Sometimes these purposes appear to be at odds. Here's a very simple overview:

Most of us have heard about our *reptilian brain*, in which pre-patterned motivations related to rituals, territoriality, and basic instincts appear to arise out of hardwired neurons whose patterns were laid down millions of years ago. Coded within this primitive part of the brain are the mechanisms for temperature control, fight-or-flight responses, and hunger. These were the skills needed in early animals for basic survival—skills that still are necessary for us.

On top of our reptilian brain is our *limbic brain*, which is associated with social group behavior, instinct and nurturing, mutual reciprocity, and other mammalian-type behaviors. These were the skills needed as animals evolved into groups and had to countermand lower instincts to compete with everything else (including our kin) for survival. Here, survival was enhanced by getting along with others. This portion of the brain is believed to be where our feelings arise, as well as the source of mood, memory, and hormone control.

On top of the limbic brain is our *neocortex*, an area present in more advanced mammals, where the complex thought processes evolved. This evolution came much later in our human development. Even now, some areas of the neocortex do not fully develop until we move into adulthood. It is this area of the brain that can plan, model, and simulate. It is where reasoning arises, and is the source of language.

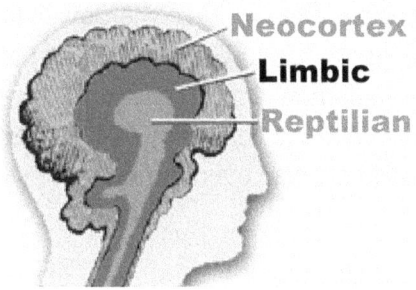

The neocortex is divided into two halves, the left and right brain hemispheres. The left hemisphere primarily is responsible for our capability to engage in analytical thought, verbal and written communication, logic, reason, mathematics, and science. The right hemisphere appears to be involved with functions such as intuition, empathy, creative expression, art, music, and holistic thought.

As we consider that we live in the world of the physical, it helps us to remember the evolutionary development of our brains and their specialized functions. These capacities have served our evolutionary past, allowing us to meet basic physical needs, band together in social groups, and develop higher mental skills such as discernment. Yet, these roles can be at odds with one another and can serve to limit our future growth.

Consider that our reptilian brain is concerned with personal survival, while our limbic brain is concerned with functioning in groups. We want to be alone, and we want to be with others. We may feel called to love someone and be with them, yet experience moments in our relationship where we are threatened and want to flee or fight.

Consider that our reptilian brain and testosterone levels push us to fulfill a need for sex, while our neocortex may apply reason to temper our physical desires or point out their inappropriateness in a particular moment.

We may believe that we have the power to control our thoughts and limit our lower brain's impulses, but that can be easier said than done. This conflict becomes even more apparent when we consider what happens when our hardwired desires meet an overabundance of what we want.

Supernormal Stimuli

Our physical evolutionary past was filled with the inability to meet certain needs whose fulfillment we now take for granted. Early humanity spent a lot of time focused on basic needs. High-fat foods were a luxury. Fattening our bodies was a useful survival tool for moving through times when food was scarce. Access to sexual partners was frequently limited.

Our life in the physical world has evolved within us mechanisms that favor and seek those things that are both beneficial and in short supply. The problem is that as humanity has evolved its technology, it has created the ability to increase the supply of the things we are evolutionarily hardwired to desire. We still are motivated by the needs of our ancestors that hunted and gathered.

Animal biologist Nikolaas Tinbergen came up with the term "supernormal stimuli" to describe the phenomenon where primitive instincts will more strongly pull animals toward *imitations* of things they need than the real thing, when those imitations exaggerate the characteristics we are hardwired to prefer. The classic example is the geese that will sit on a soccer ball and neglect their real eggs. They are thought to be favoring the bigger egg with the greater chance of survival.[4]

Evolutionary psychologist Deirdre Barrett has used this concept to explore the alarming disconnect between human instinct and our created environment. In her book, *Supernormal Stimuli,* she describes how these higher stimuli are a major cause of some of today's most pressing problems, such as our tendency toward obesity and the growing addiction to Internet porn.[5]

In times past, we could not obtain access to all the food we wanted. Now we can. We also are hardwired to want the high-fat foods that will get us through the lean times, even though there are no more such lean times in developed nations. Yet, we continue to crave fatty foods, preferring them over leaner foods even as we physically grow fatter and fatter.

In times past, a man had limited opportunities to experience women sexually. He is hardwired to take advantage of the limited opportunities that make themselves available, so as to reproduce. The only problem is that desire to take advantage of every opportunity for sex is met by the opportunity to experience sexual gratification continuously in modern life. For some, this hardwired desire can override any conscious attempts not to be consumed by sex.

To be clear, there are other psychological factors that

contribute to a person being drawn into addictions to food, sex, drugs, and other things that our bodies may be evolutionarily predisposed toward. However, the point I want you to consider here is that although we may aspire to a higher outcome in our life, there may be physical forces redirecting those aspirations. Once again, we see that we are living simultaneously in two worlds.

Maslow's Hierarchy

As we consider that we live concurrently in both a physical and a metaphysical world, nothing brings that point more into focus than the pioneering work of Abraham Maslow and his "hierarchy of needs." Many of us are familiar with this theory.

Consider this: Why do you do the things you do each day? Have you ever stopped to consider it? Why is one thing more important to you than another? Why do the things that matter to you seem to change from moment to moment in some cases, while other motivators seem to change more slowly?

I didn't think too much about any of this in my younger days; those bigger questions just weren't on my mind. Yes, I recall some moments where, as a child, I lay in the grass, looking up at the clouds and wondering where God was, or how high up you had to go to see heaven. Most of the time I was more concerned with fitting in with my group of buddies or trying to get some girl to like me. As it turns out, that's basically normal. When Swiss psychologist Jean Piaget mapped the stages of childhood development, he discovered that we don't develop the kind of abstract thinking necessary for asking for such questions until late childhood, or sometimes even adulthood.

I recall that I was eighteen and had just arrived at college when I felt the first inklings of the desire to figure out who I was and why I thought the way I did. In my first semester, I took an introduction to psychology class and discovered that I had all the symptoms of every type of abnormal psychological diagnosis in the textbook! I ended up majoring in psychology partly as an attempt to cure myself.

Now I can admit that many of the psychological theories I read about at that time were either over my head or just didn't seem to have much applicability in the real world. My university's psychology department was very much into B.F. Skinner and behavioralism, so I read a lot about that subject. At one point, I was working for a professor who was putting implants in rats' skulls and running experiments on the effects of electrical stimulation on parts of their brains. The experiments involved a lot of stimulus-response ideas that didn't seem to apply to me.

Then I discovered the work of Abraham Maslow and his "hierarchy." Finally, I'd found a theory that answered many of the questions I had been asking about myself. What initially appealed to me about Maslow was that instead of focusing on humans performing abnormally, he sought and studied high performers and asked what motivated them. More importantly, I saw how his theory could be applied in the real world.

As a professor at Brooklyn College, New York, in the late 1930s and 1940s, Maslow was in the perfect place to study those who were exhibiting high mental health. He began observing and noting the characteristics of fellow professors and mentors, looking for common denominators among those individuals. This process started a lifelong pursuit of seeking the universal human indicators of self-actualizing performance. One of the most famous subjects that Maslow observed was Albert Einstein.[6]

As Maslow tracked the characteristics of high-performing humans, he noted that there was a trend or direction in their traits and that their motivators that could be mapped. Ultimately, he created his basic theory, which he outlined in the 1943 paper, "A Theory of Human Motivation." His theory detailed five basic categories of human motivators or needs.[7] Only later was the visual image of a pyramid employed to illustrate the hierarchical nature of his theory.

According to Maslow's theory, each of these five levels of motivators can be stacked so that one is on top of another, with our lower or basic needs on the bottom and our higher needs on the top. The theory says that fulfilling one level allows us to move up to the next. If, at any time, a lower-level need is no longer being met, we are plunged back down to the lower need, which must be met again before we can return to being concerned about the higher need.

The following diagram provides a brief summary of the five levels of Maslow's original hierarchy of needs:

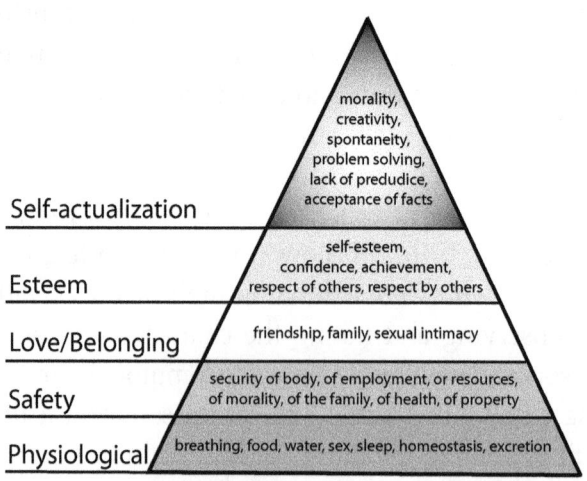

Our basic, primary motivators are our physiological needs—water, air, food, and sleep—which are essential for our bodily survival. Maslow stated that once these needs are met, we can be concerned with our security needs—shelter from the elements, a steady job, and a sense that life around us is stable and secure. Meeting these needs allows us to focus next on our social needs—feeling that we are loved, that we belong to our group, that we have secure relationships, and that we feel accepted. Meeting our social needs allows us to focus on what Maslow termed "self-esteem" needs—a feeling of importance, social recognition, and feeling worthy. Finally, at the pinnacle of Maslow's pyramid was what he called our desire for "self-actualization": fulfilling our highest potential, seeking personal growth for its own sake, and moving beyond being concerned with the opinions of others.

Although Maslow's model appears nice and neat, life is not always that way. The needs motivating our actions in a particular moment can be dynamic, shifting between levels so quickly that it may be hard to determine which level is actually driving us. Yet, from the moment I first encountered Maslow's idea and his pyramid, it has always resonated with me. It rings true from my experience, both in college and throughout my life.

Later in his life, Maslow expanded upon his basic theory in two ways. First, he realized he could place all his need levels into two groups: "deficiency" needs and "being" needs.[8] Deficiency needs are driven by a sense of *lack* in our lives. When we are lacking something, it places us in survival mode—we must obtain it. If we have it, and someone tries to take it away from us, we will fight for it. "Being" needs arise not from lack, but from a sense of fullness and a desire to grow. Rather than living with a sense of lack, we sense that we have more than enough of what we need and want to share our abundance. Our "being" needs are about thriving and moving into the highest potential of who we can be.

Simply stated, lower needs are about survival; higher needs are about thriving.

Secondly, Maslow added three more categories of "needs" he had identified. Between the levels of self-esteem and self-actualization in his early work, he added a "desire to understand" and a "desire for aesthetic beauty." He also realized that self-actualization should be divided into two levels: his original self-actualization and a higher need that he termed a "desire for transcendence"—an inner pull to move beyond the physical, human experience.

As he acquired more data and was able to better analyze the nature of human needs, Maslow "evolved" in his understanding of those needs. The evolution of his theory led to a recognition that as we meet our physical needs, we become more motivated by metaphysical needs.

If we apply this idea to our own lives, we can recognize that there is a shift occurring within us. On the one hand, we are still tied to our evolutionary past and animalistic temperament. Our lower brain, hormones, DNA, physical body, and basic needs still direct many of our actions. On the other hand, our higher brain and higher needs are emerging, based on new world conditions calling us to higher expressions of ourselves.

This information is useful as we seek to use our free-will choice to move our lives forward. During times when we consciously *choose* to focus on higher needs, other thoughts and desires from our subjective consciousness may be choosing differently. Recognizing this potential internal conflict brings it into our awareness, so we can consciously choose to ensure that our animalistic and subjective needs are appropriately met and are not undermining our higher-level, conscious choices.

The fact that we all have to deal with this dual nature is important information for us to keep in mind as we deal with other humans. You, I, and everyone we meet lives in these two worlds simultaneously. Recognizing that fact opens us to a greater understanding of the motivations of others, enabling us to express compassion and acceptance when their needs differ from ours.

Directing Consciousness

One final way I'd like to call attention to how we humans are all alike is through the power of our consciousness and choosing our thoughts. I've already touched upon this briefly several times.

In my story of my nanny Lolete, we can see how the power of consciousness can lead to the creation of certain experiences in our lives. In my young awareness, I internalized a belief that something was wrong with me. My parents did not intend for me to create this belief due to their actions. For much of my life, I was not consciously aware that I held this belief. Yet, like it or not, I created experiences based on this hidden thought.

I can recall starting first grade in my new town and feeling somehow inadequate compared to my fellow first-graders. I was too tall. I was not attractive enough. I was not smart enough. I was not worthy of having the kids I perceived as "cool" as my friends. Hence, I had few friends and none of them were "cool." I was one of the last kids to be picked when we chose teams to play kickball at school. I frequently played alone on the playground.

When we moved to another city in the middle of my third-grade year, my feelings of being an outcast grew. I had a crush on a young girl down the street, but felt there was no way I could act upon those feelings. During the three years we lived just a few houses from one another, I never lost the feelings and I never told her I had them. I believed I wasn't good enough.

My point is not to get you to feel sympathy for me; I did have friends and a substantial degree of childhood "success." Eventually, I overcame this hidden and mistaken belief. My point is that within my consciousness, to a degree in my awareness and to a degree invisible to me, was the belief that in certain aspects of life I was not worthy of what I desired—and that belief kept me from attaining it. My thoughts created my reality.

So, do our thoughts create our reality? The popularity in recent years of the book and the movie *The Secret* have brought this question more into the public's awareness and have led to some emotional debates.[9]

Proponents of the "law of attraction" offer their own life experience as proof that it works. Opponents do the same. Most people, if they are truly honest with themselves, can point to situations where they affirmed something was going to happen and it did—and where it didn't.

So, where does that leave us? Generally, it leaves proponents explaining away situations where the law of attraction appeared not to work, and opponents dismissing it as a law because it appeared not to work consistently, 100 percent of the time.

Personally, I have experienced a great deal of validity regarding the law of attraction. It has been my experience that when it appeared to not work, it was because I misinterpreted the law. Some people that hear of this law think it means that if they simply focus their intention on something, it will occur. What is lost in that interpretation is the interconnectedness of everything: What one person "wants" may not be the highest outcome for the whole of life. The appearance that the law of attraction did not work may be because, at a higher level, the collective needs of humanity were better served by a different outcome—or the higher needs of my individual life were better served by a different outcome (for example, so I could learn something

I needed to learn). It also could be the case that I really did not believe something I thought I believed.

Yet, if you are a critic of the law of attraction, you probably are thinking I am one the proponents trying to "explain away" the times it didn't work. Ultimately, it's okay with me if you dismiss the law of attraction entirely. Whether this "law" is truly a law is not the point I want you to focus on now. Rather, I want you to recognize that there is power in where we focus our attention. This control can be so ubiquitous and invisible that we tend to forget it's even there.

For now, I simply want you to remember that everything you have ever deliberately created started first with a thought in your mind. When you raise your arm, you first thought about raising your arm. You thought about going out to dinner, and then you did. Everything is created twice—first in consciousness, and then in your life.

Now, you might mention all your autonomic bodily functions and say you didn't think about making your heart beat, your food digest, your hair grow, and so on. It's true that these functions continue beautifully without your conscious awareness. However, as you will recall, the way I am defining consciousness includes your subconscious nature, which incorporates the intelligence inherent in your body and its cells. So for the moment, simply consider that below the level of your awareness, your cells "thought" to run these functions.

Some of you may be conjuring up other examples to debate my point. For even the strict materialist who hears the words "your thoughts create your reality" and immediately starts to debate what I'm expressing, I invite you to momentarily set aside your objections. Instead, acknowledge to at least some degree how many aspects of your life do begin based on a conscious thought you had. Keep in mind that it's not about thinking something and then sitting back and waiting for it to happen—it's about thinking something and following up with all the actions within your sphere of influence that will move you toward that "something." That's a process sequence that I think all of us can agree upon.

The bottom line is: What we give our time and energy to in life is what tends to grow in our life. Withdrawing our time and energy from something causes it to shrivel up from disregard.

The more I practice the piano, the better I get at it. The more I focus on my job and career, the more success I have. The more I neglect my body by failing to focus on my diet and exercise, the fatter and unhealthier I become. The less I focus on the relationships in my life, the more they wither and struggle.

Here's an example: For several years my wife and I would talk about our desire to travel to Europe. Year after year, we never went. We had the thought, but it never manifested. At one point, we decided to put more energy into it. We bought travel books, did research on the Internet, and began asking others for advice. The energy we devoted into planning eventually led to action—taking time off from work, booking our trip, and actually going!

I begin each day by creating a list of the things I'm going to do that day. In other words, I *think* of what I want to create, and then I follow that thinking with *action* to create it. Some days I'm more successful than others. On those days, my actions are more in alignment with my thoughts. On days when I am less successful, I realize that I have allowed distractions to get in my way. My actions have not been in alignment with my thoughts.

Everything in our life begins with our thoughts; our words and actions follow them.

So if this process works in our individual lives, what about the power of our collective intentions? What if we all intended the same thing? It turns out that there is a lot of evidence to support the power of collective intention. Author and researcher Lynne McTaggart and many others have written extensively on this subject.[10]

For now, I want to keep this discussion in an area that most of us can agree upon. If I have a thought about creating something and then act upon that thought, and you have a similar thought and start acting upon it, the combination of the two of us working toward the same goal increases the chances that it will come about. The more people that are in alignment with an intention in their mind, followed up by coordinated action, the greater the result in the world. This is the power of teamwork, simply stated. Most of us believe in the power of teams to accomplish great things.

So, can you agree for the moment that your thoughts have some power over where your life goes? Can you also agree that each of us can direct our lives for our personal betterment? Finally, can you possibly see how, by each of us choosing the best for our lives in a manner that also is in alignment with the best for humanity, we can address the current challenges facing us? I hope so. Then, the question becomes, *How do we harness this power of our directed thinking to solve problems facing humanity, to take the higher path at the evolutionary crossroads?*

Certainly, if there is power in individual intentions and even greater power in teams that come together with shared intentions, there is hope that we can foster cooperation around a set of common desires and create a world that works for everyone.

Our Current Challenge—Differences in Consciousness

Why are we struggling with things that we are all in agreement are issues that humanity must transcend? Consider the problems of war, poverty, disease, overpopulation, overuse of the resources of Earth, climate change, lack of availability of clean water, lack of access to inexpensive renewable energy, and more. Why does it seem that we cannot use the power of the directed consciousness of multiple individuals—teams focusing on the same goal—to solve these concerns?

If you consider this question, you might come up with a list of barriers to our successful solution of these problems through the use of directed teams. The potential problems likely could be reduced to these two issues: lack of agreement that there is actually a problem, and lack of agreement on the solution.

Why is there this lack of agreement? Although there are many reasons, I'll reduce it to one: our different worldviews, which were outlined previously. Your solution to each of the issues (or even the idea that there is a problem that needs to be solved) will differ based upon whether your back story is traditional, materialistic or humanistic.

To see how people with different worldviews can view an issue differently, let's look at one example: the economic crisis of 2008 and beyond.

When we consider our lack of agreement on how to deal with this issue, the media tends to present it to us as the story of conservative Republicans that favor deregulating business versus liberal Democrats that favor regulating business. They tell us that the "right" (conservative group) wants to avoid raising taxes in any situation. The right holds the belief that taxing corporations and the wealthy prevents them from creating jobs. Conversely, we are told that the "left" (liberal group) seeks to tax the wealthy in an attempt to bring some degree of social equity. The right believes that unions have inhibited business growth and seeks to restrict them; the left believes that unions serve to protect people from abuses of corporations. Can this issue be seen in a way other than "left versus right"? How would each of the three worldviews potentially view this issue?

A traditional worldview seeks to keep the status quo, supporting the American dream that anyone can become rich. The idea that "we don't want to limit the ability of the successful to create their profits" is part of this American dream. The tradition is that there have always been wealthy, powerful people, and there have always been poor people. From the perspective of this worldview, we don't want to do anything that upsets this system. We should keep the taxes of the rich low and minimize regulations for companies. The best government is the one that is least involved in the economic system. The traditional viewpoint also loves to create black-and-white rules. Our religious doctrines, as well as our first legal systems, came from the traditional viewpoint. Hence, this way of looking at life would value having their politicians sign pledges that clearly declare, up front, their position on issues such as taxes, and that limit them from bending these clear-cut rules.

A materialist worldview values the ability of businesses and people to work to achieve maximum profits. In this view, each of us is here on Earth to get as much material wealth as possible. We have invested in corporations and want the best return on our investments. We work for personal self-gain. There is nothing wrong with companies and people maximizing how much they get.

A materialist recognizes the importance of all of the parts of our "economic engine" being well-oiled and working smoothly. They value collecting data and adjusting the system as necessary to ensure our economic viability. Such adjustments can include appropriate regulations as well as economic stimulus payments to banks and other companies to keep the system working. The government plays a useful role in ensuring the success of all aspects of the economy. Those that hold this worldview keep in mind the phrase, "It's the economy, stupid"—that life is about continuous growth of the economy.

The humanistic worldview would value the needs of people over corporations, seeing businesses as tools for humans to use to drive a successful society. From this viewpoint, profits are a useful motivation for businesses to provide services and innovations. Ultimately, the system is designed to serve humans and meet their needs. Too much inequity in the distribution of wealth does not serve the needs of the people. The system should serve all people, not just the wealthy. Government plays a vital role in ensuring that the overall system is working—not so much to ensure the balance between people and corporations, which drives the materialistic view, but to ensure that the system is providing an adequate standard of living for all people. The idea is that people be kept safe, physically and economically, by the workings of companies and corporations.

Hopefully by now you are starting to comprehend the picture I'm painting. It's likely that we could debate some of the details I've offered about how the various worldviews might look at this issue, but such details are not important here. What is primary is that you understand how worldviews might be at play in our disagreements regarding how to use the power of our collective, directive thought to solve these issues. As long as our "back stories" are invisibly guiding our thoughts, our collective thinking will be at odds with those holding another worldview.

Humans have evolved along a path where it was advantageous to break things down into two categories: good versus bad, beneficial versus harmful, fight versus flight. In the past, rapidly making distinctions and categorizations frequently saved our lives. The fittest survived by making quick choices between two categories.

Famed Russian biologist Ivan Pavlov coined the term "orienting response" for our hardwired tendency to direct our senses toward a new stimulus that appears in our environment. We freeze for a few seconds, the blood vessels in the brain dilate, our muscles constrict, our heart slows, and our alpha brain waves are momentarily blocked. This response leads us to pause and quickly determine if the new stimulus is a potential predator, possible prey, or likely mate. Our survival and success was dependent upon this response and our quick summary of the situation.[11]

Our propensity for either/or kinds of things is obvious in our media and politics, where issues and ideas typically are reduced to two simple categories. We considered this idea earlier, in the debate over evolution.

The problem is that modern life is more complex than two categories allow for. There are multiple sides to every issue, and the various aspects intermingle. Using the two-category approach, we end up trying to put square pegs into round holes.

As American media presents a choice between left-versus-right perspectives, and American political parties present a choice between Republicans and Democrats, many of us viewing life from the traditional, materialistic, and humanistic viewpoints can't determine which perspective or party best represents them. We choose one or the other that seems the "best fit" on factors from our worldview that are most important to us at the moment.

Presently, humanity is at a major crossroads. Behind us is our historical path, our animalistic history—a world driven by survival of the fittest. It is a world of violence and scarcity, where all humans are in competition for limited resources. Some of us will emerge as winners; most will end up as losers with little opportunity. This is the world that created our lower brain, and the world our lower brain seeks to live in. This is the world where we live motivated by our deficiency needs, approaching matters from a continuous sense of lack. We seek to survive.

In front of us is our highest vision of what we can be—our spiritual future. It is a world driven by peace and prosperity, where all humans are valued and have the opportunity to express themselves and succeed. This is the world our higher brain evolved into, and brought into existence. This is the world where we live motivated by our "being" needs, where we approach things from a continuous sense of abundance. We seek to thrive.

How is this movement from *survive* to *thrive* being experienced? We are moving through the birthing canal from our animal nature to our spiritual nature via the pains humanity is going through at this time.

Our desire to simply survive is bringing about growing conflicts between different ideologies, increasing economic disparity, competition over converting others to our way of thinking, and battles for control of our social systems. All these conflicts seem to shift between battling for our minds and battling for our possessions. We have culture wars on our left, and battles between the haves and have-nots on our right.

Our fight for survival leads us into wars, political stalemates, and economic battles. Companies seek to control governments to set the rules to maximize corporate profits. Politicians give in to monetary interest. Military actions are driven less by the needs of the country and more by the needs of the military-industrial complex and the wealthy. The "fittest" are the richest, who seek to use their advantages to become even richer and more "fit."

Yet, even as we experience all this conflict and competition, we sense a better path—a higher way, a call to thriving, a greater vision of how humanity can live together. In this elevated vision, we can picture a world that works for everyone. In such a world, all humans have their basic needs met and are afforded the opportunity to work on their self-actualization. Everyone recognizes that their role in life is to thrive, and in doing so, they assist others to thrive.

Transcending Our Current Challenge

Can we come together as a species and collectively make the choices that will bridge us to this higher vision?

Can you imagine the progress we would experience if the vast majority were aware of our evolutionary journey, agreed upon the basic tenets of our collective vision for our future, and agreed to think and act in a manner that uses the power of teamwork to move toward that vision? Such a situation would create a major leap in our collective unfoldment.

Just to be clear, I am not suggesting that we all must think alike. There is, in fact, great value in diversity of opinion, and great vulnerability when too many march together in lockstep. It is the melding of diverse ideas and beliefs that has driven the engine of humanity's creative growth. When we all think alike, the creative fertilizer of a new idea can get discarded without proper consideration. Too much sameness, coupled with unhealed aspects of our shadow, can lead to group behavior that is destructive rather than constructive. Consider Nazi Germany, or misguided cult leaders like Jim Jones (leader of the Peoples Temple tragedy in 1978) and their followers.

When humanity is inspired by its highest idea of what it can become, and a critical mass of people move toward that lofty vision while allowing for a diversity of ideas to seed the possibility of an even superior vision, evolutionary soaring can occur. Such great gains often follow periods of great pains—if we can move through the pain and learn its lessons.

Instantaneous worldwide media delivers humanity's struggles to our awareness continuously as they occur. Our consciousness is inundated with bad news; it often seems overwhelming. Behind all this is a growing sense that if we don't do something soon to solve our problems, we will pass a point of no return where humanity will move into some type of apocalyptic future. Although I suppose that's possible, my optimism sees us coming together and moving forward. We will choose a life of "heaven" over a life of "hell." The angels of our better nature are calling us forward.

As we move forward, let's all remember that the first key to crossing the bridge to our highest future is to focus on our commonalities rather than our differences. Remember that we are all alike in that each of us has the ability to direct our thinking consciously. You, I, and everyone we meet has this ability. To the degree we can come together and share this power toward a common goal—a common vision for our future—the greater our ability to bring it to fruition.

Part Three:

Visions of Our Highest Future

In the third section of the book, we will explore the following ideas:

- The second key to our crossing the bridge to our highest future is for each of us to visualize and focus on that possible future.
- Some scientists, philosophers, and mystics have described where they believe our evolution is headed.
- There are many common characteristics that we can glean from their descriptions.
- There have been attempts to bring humanity together under a common vision for the future; one such recent attempt was by the United Nations.

Scientists, Philosophers, and Mystics Ideas About Evolution's Direction

Throughout this book I have asked you to develop or enhance your ability to see life from an evolutionary perspective. As you have been using this lens, I also have asked you to consider that we are at a major milestone where we are crossing the bridge from our current crises to a better future—crossing the bridge from our competitive past to our cooperative future, crossing the bridge from our animalistic past to our spiritual future. I have encouraged you to use the power of your conscious thoughts to focus upon our greatest possible future.

The next logical question becomes, "What is that future?" What do we mean by a better future, a cooperative future, or a spiritual future? And, who gets to define it?

The Greeks used the word *telos* to describe the ultimate "end, goal, purpose, or final cause" of something. *Teleology* is the philosophical study of these end purposes. Humans have long gazed into the future to determine where we are headed.

Most scientists don't like to make predictions about the future. Science is, after all, about empirical measurements and observations—creating theories, testing them, and revising them accordingly. We use the scientific method to understand the workings of the material world so that we can better manipulate it. Scientific understanding does lead to future predictions (consider weather forecasts as an obvious example), but most scientists are very reluctant to use their data to suggest any ultimate endgame.

Yet, there have been some individuals steeped in science (both the physical and social sciences) that have offered some clues. Moreover, many philosophers have suggested where our future path may be headed. The topic frequently surfaces in the intuitive wisdom offered by mystics.

So, where *are* we headed? There are a number of these sources that appear to be in general agreement about our ultimate evolutionary destination; let's look at a few briefly. Yes, I did selectively choose the ones presented here. Obviously my worldview and bias enters into all of this book! My cherry-picking a side, you will no doubt find the commonalities interesting.

As you read through these ideas, try to identify common themes.

Maslow

Abraham Maslow, whose ideas we have already explored, offers the idea that as we all are able to meet our basic deficiency needs, we will then move into working toward our "being" needs of self-actualization and self-transcendence. In other words, our evolutionary direction is toward becoming all that we can be in this individual lifetime and then moving into the realm of seeing how our life is connected to something greater that is beyond us as an individual.

Maslow observed, "All the evidence that we have indicates that it is reasonable to assume in practically every human being, and certainly in almost every newborn baby, that there is an active will toward health, an impulse towards growth, or towards the actualization."

What exactly is "self-actualization"?

Some of the characteristics Maslow listed as being

indicative of a self-actualizing individual include:

- Being concerned with solving problems that are greater than the individual.
- The need for independence and autonomy.
- Having peak experiences that allow glimpses of the greater possibilities of life.
- Experiencing the world with awe and wonder.
- Being able to follow rules, yet being open to new ways and new possibilities.
- Recognizing that life is more about the journey than about the destination.[12]

Next, what exactly does Maslow mean by "self-transcendence"?

Some of the characteristics that Maslow listed as being indicative of individual he termed "transcenders" include:

- They have certain peak experiences that connect them to something outside of their individual self, and this connection becomes one of the most important things in their lives.
- They speak more easily, normally, naturally, and unconsciously the language of *being*—the language of poets, mystics, seers, and profoundly religious individuals.
- They perceive the sacredness in all things while simultaneously perceiving them at the practical, everyday level.
- They have a "holistic" view of the world.
- They exhibit a strengthening of the self-actualizer's natural tendency to synergy—intra-psychic, interpersonal, intra-culturally, and internationally;

there is a transcendence of competitiveness and zero-sum (win-lose) gamesmanship.
- There is more and easier transcendence of the ego, the self, and the identity.
- They seem spontaneously to prefer simplicity and to avoid luxury, privilege, honors, and possessions.
- They are more apt to regard themselves as carriers of talent—instruments of the transpersonal, temporary custodians of a greater intelligence, skill, leadership, or efficiency.[13]

In the description of these characteristics, we see an individual clearly driven by a desire to make a difference on the planet. We see someone who is called to a greater purpose, to serve the greater good through their own unique abilities. We see someone who wants the freedom to follow their passion and hone their skills so they can enjoy life's journey and make it better for others. We see someone who is motivated to experience firsthand their connectedness to something beyond their small self.

Pink

Contemporary author Daniel Pink has come to a similar conclusion in outlining what he called our human "Motivation 2.0" in his bestselling book, *Drive*. According to Pink, the old methods of trying to motivate people are no longer effective. Rather than trying to change the behavior of others with external motivators such as grades, scores, higher pay, and the like, he says there is growing evidence that what truly motivates people are internal factors. He outlines three essential elements to his motivational outline.

First is what he calls *autonomy*—being motivated by the desire to direct our own lives. When we are told what to do, or directed by others in some way, it is a motivation killer. When we are given the option to direct our own path and make our own choices, it drives us forward.

Second is what he calls *mastery*—being motivated by an urge to continuously improve our performance at something that truly matters to us. Whatever is calling us in life to do it, we are motivated to get better at it.

Third is what he calls *purpose*—being motivated by a desire to be of service to a higher purpose that is much bigger in scope than we believe our individual lives to be. There is a major goal calling us to serve it, and that goal is meeting some larger aspect for humanity and ourselves.

Pink suggests that, increasingly, we are being motivated by autonomy, mastery, and purpose. We want to make our own choices, and generally will choose to do our best at something that provides us purpose in life.[14]

Covey

Stephen Covey was a business guru best known for his book, *The 7 Habits of Highly Effective People* , in which he presented the seven "habits" he discovered by studying effective leaders and identifying their common characteristics. Although Covey wrote a number of other books, only one was put forth as a true sequel to his classic book. Fifteen years later, he came out with *The 8th Habit: From Effectiveness to Greatness*.

It was only after Covey's own growth that he had the realization that greatness is "greater" than effectiveness. It's my interpretation that Covey is telling us that our own personal growth is ultimately moving each of us toward greatness. What do we do when we are mastering the habit of "greatness"? According to Covey, greatness beckons us to find our unique voice or calling (our reason for being here), to express it fully, and then to assist everyone else in finding their voice and conveying it to the world. In other words, *to be great is to be ourselves at our highest level*—and in doing so, to help others attain their highest potential.[15]

Holmes

Ernest Holmes was a twentieth-century philosopher who, by studying science, philosophy, and religion, created his own life philosophy called the Science of Mind and Spirit. In this philosophy, Holmes says that each person is an individual expression of God or Spirit—but this is not the old model of a God separate from us. Rather, we were born out of a Oneness of Spirit to have our experiences and growth here on Earth. As a part of this process, we "forgot" that we came from the Oneness.

This separation allows us the free-will choice to decide what we will think and do as we move through life. As we choose and think, we create our lives. Sometimes we choose wisely; sometimes we don't. Some of our choices obviously are not in alignment with this true unity (that is, we may choose to do harmful things to ourselves and others). However, at the level of our unity, we cannot harm or destroy our eternal and universal nature—the Oneness is not affected by our ignorance. We move through these life experiences for the experience and learning they provide to us. Ultimately, evolution becomes a process whereby our life experiences return us to awareness of the unity of all.

Within this context, Holmes says that we are pushed by the internal force of love to connect with others, and that we are pulled by a unique "divine urge" within us to express some specific talent more fully. Both of these forces call us out from the sense of being separate and apart from one another and back into a realization that we are all connected. Hence, our evolutionary path is moving us through our experience of being separate individuals, and back into our sense of unity or oneness.[16].

Spiral Dynamics

Spiral Dynamics is a scientific theory derived from the work of Dr. Claire Graves in the early 1970s, but it did not become well-known until the late 1990s. Similar to Maslow, Graves first developed his theory of human development based on his years of research into understanding the higher reaches of human nature. He employed different techniques for measuring people's values over a period of years.

As he analyzed his data, he recognized certain key points: (1) that we all appear to move through a common sequence of worldviews; (2) that our worldviews emerge to meet the needs of our current life conditions; (3) as we meet our current life conditions, we begin to experience the emergence of new life conditions; and (4) the new life conditions call forth the emergence of a new worldview that is appropriate for that environment. Graves's ideas were key in our previous discussion of our personal back stories and worldviews.

Mapping the sequence of these worldviews allowed Graves (and us) to see the pattern of humanity's past as well as the "higher" or more recent worldviews that have emerged. Individuals are born into the "lower"-level worldviews and grow or develop into the "higher" worldviews, settling into the one most appropriate for their life's conditions. Similarly, we can look back over the history of humanity and recognize that these "lower" worldviews developed early in our planetary history and that the "higher" ones developed later, as we made advancements in our technology that enhanced our life situation. If we track these sets of values to determine which ones appeared later in our history, we can gain a potential indication of where the human race may be headed.

Graves tracked a series of six worldviews, which he considered the basic ones that have served humanity until now. The earliest one dealt with basic survival needs. The second one emerged during the development of the earliest tribes, where we first developed myths about life in an attempt to understand it. Third was our worldview that allowed power to rest with a few at the expense of others, and where kings protected their servants. The next three worldviews were the ones we described previously, which are still playing out in Western culture: the traditionalists, materialists, and humanists (although Spiral Dynamics gives them different names). According to Graves, one thing all of these first six viewpoints have in common is that any individual that has these viewpoints is unaware of the existence or validity of any of the other ways of seeing life. Each worldview believes their worldview is the only one.

Graves then described what he saw as a small but emerging "second tier" of worldviews that, for the first time, showed humans as being capable of becoming aware of the existence of all other worldviews and, more importantly, allowing them to recognize each worldview's validity in meeting humanity's needs at that stage of our development. As individuals evolved to this second tier, they recognized this evolutionary path of viewpoints that humans had developed to meet their needs, seeing that there was a perfection and utility in each of the viewpoints, which have served humanity through all the various phases of human experience.

Individuals that develop this awareness can observe all the worldviews around them (for us, these are primarily the traditional, materialistic, and humanistic ones) and see that individuals who are living from that point of view are not "wrong"; they simply have adopted a set of beliefs that are appropriate for their life and their culture. The model shows us that these viewpoints are not static, but continually evolve as new life conditions emerge. As individuals and groups in the traditional worldview meet their challenges, they are open to moving into the materialistic viewpoint. As the materialistic conditions are met, the humanistic viewpoint can emerge. As the humanistic conditions are met, they can leap into the second-tier "integral" consciousness that is able to integrate all the levels.

As Graves tracked the individuals who made this leap to the newly emerging worldview, he found a number of common characteristics. From an evolutionary standpoint, we might consider that this is where we all might be going if we are able to master our current conditions.

Among the characteristics of individuals who move into these "higher" levels are the following:

- We recognize the value of all the worldviews and how they have served an evolutionary process.
- We see life as an interplay of systems of complexity that interact upon each other and drive us to higher levels of complexity.
- We sense the inner melding of science and spirituality.

- We move toward an understanding of the power of our minds and expand our use of consciousness though employing brain and mind tools.
- We sense that the role of the individual is to serve a larger conscious, spiritual whole.
- We become more motivated to assume our role of service to the entire spiral of life.[17]

Wilber and Integral

Similar to Holmes, philosopher Ken Wilber has studied science, philosophy, and religion, looking for common threads of truth. The information he derived from various sources led him to create his "integral" philosophical model, which plots his findings onto a kind of "map" to see what new insights they may offer. Although the theory can be used in a number of ways, here we simply will consider what the theory says about our evolutionary destination.

Integral theory points out that we are evolving upward in various multiple intelligences (cognitive, social, spiritual, etcetera) within the inner world of our consciousness and culture, as well as the outer world of our bodies, technology, and social systems. Wilber describes what he calls "20 tenets of evolution," of which several relate to its *telos* (a purpose or ending that something is moving toward). Among his tenets is a recognition that we are moving toward increasing complexity and autonomy, among other factors[18].

Additionally, Wilber says that, "Evolution goes beyond what went before, but because it must embrace what went before, then its very nature is to transcend and include, and thus it has an inherent directionality, a secret impulse, toward increasing depth, increasing intrinsic value, increasing consciousness."

Wilber points out that the evolutionary process involves entities that are "whole and complete" by themselves (he uses the term *holons*), to be transcended yet included in the next whole and complete holon up the evolutionary chain. As such, atoms are transcended and included within molecules, molecules are transcended and included within cells, cells are transcended and included within small organisms, and so on. The movement up the chain of "transcending and including" occurs in greater and greater "depth." And, as consciousness is in all (consciousness is the "ground of all being"), as we move up in "depth," there is a greater and greater "consciousness."

Wilber describes a spiritual path that involves both *descending* and *ascending*. Similar to Holmes, Wilber says that the "One" emptied itself into all its creation, and that this was the descent of the One into the Many. The great diversity in the world is seen as part of the Goodness of the Divine. We are called to have compassion and care for the multiplicity of expressions through the power of *agape*—love that reaches out to embrace all. At the same time, we are drawn up a "path of ascent" from the Many to the One. As we gain wisdom, we see behind all the various forms and phenomena that there is only the One. One of the forces that moves us up this path is the upward pull of love or Eros.

Simply stated, integral theory suggests that we came from the One to experience a sense of separation, but that evolutionary forces (including love) are evolving us back into a sense of unity. As we evolve, we have greater and greater levels of "consciousness."

Stewart

There are those who believe there is a direction to evolution that can be acknowledged without moving into the realm of the mystics and spirituality. One such individual is John Stewart, who writes, "The trajectory of evolution is not produced by an external force, or by some impulse that is intrinsic to the universe, or by an ideal end-point that somehow attracts evolution towards it. Directionality can be explained and understood fully without resort to mysticism."

Stewart wrote the book, *Evolution's Arrow*, a detailed look at the physical processes of evolution, and he concluded that there is a developmental route we are moving toward. He acknowledges that his conclusions are not generally shared by most current evolutionary writers.

Stewart uses the bulk of his book to demonstrate that evolution is progressive, producing increasing cooperation among living processes. Most evolutionary scientists acknowledge that cooperation has been a key method employed in physical development, but that such cooperation is employed only when it favors the underlying motive of the "selfish" genes that seek to replicate themselves. According to Stewart, "Evolution progresses towards greater cooperation by discovering ways to build cooperative organizations out of components that are self-interested." He points out that it was cooperative groups of self-replicating molecular processes that formed the first cells. It was the ability of these cells to find a way to cooperate that allowed them to become multi-cellular organisms, cooperative insect societies, and such complex entities as human social systems.

Interestingly, he states that, "The potential for further beneficial cooperation will not be finally exhausted until all living processes are permanently organized into a single entity that is of the largest possible scale. The potential for increases in the scale of cooperation in this universe will end only when the entire universe is subsumed in a single, unified cooperative organization of living processes."

Another attribute that Stewart sees as increasing as evolution proceeds is something called *evolvability*, the ability to evolve successfully through the discovery of effective adaptations. To put it another way, in early stages of evolutionary development, successful adaptations were a matter of randomness or luck, just as most materialist scientists would point out. Some mutation occurred that produced an attribute more favorable for the current environment, leading to the birth of more offspring carrying that trait.

However, Stewart suggests that as we move up the evolutionary path, higher development brings greater learning. Learning brings the ability to make a change in our current lifetime immediately by way of choice. The greater our ability to read the present environment and make immediate adaptations, the more we are exhibiting evolvability.

Stewart sees humanity as being at an interesting fork in the road—one where we "must find better ways to build evolvable cooperative societies if we are to participate successfully in the future evolution of life in the universe."

Part of our current challenge is our difficulty in expanding beyond certain degrees of selfishness and moving to higher cooperative stages. One example Stewart cites as evidence of this selfish behavior is how the unequal distribution of wealth allows the rich to manipulate the media, as well as our political parties and our government, so as to contribute to their accumulation of even more wealth.

Ultimately, Stewart calls us to develop what he calls "evolutionary awareness." He says, "Evolutionary awareness shows us that it is an illusion to see ourselves or other individuals as distinct and separate entities. Individuals are inextricably part of an ongoing evolutionary process." If we can develop this type of awareness, we realize that our pursuit of many of our selfish interests (such as money, sex, power, etcetera) leads to a wasted life. *Meaning* comes from contributing to humanity's greater evolution.

What can we do to contribute to the future evolutionary success of life on Earth? Stewart offers us three objectives. First, grow our personal adaptability and evolvability. We do that by developing our self-knowledge and psychological skills so we can transcend our biological and cultural past. Similar to Maslow, he encourages us to no longer be controlled by our biological and cultural needs, noting that we are now finding our motivation in something higher. Second, he encourages us to promote to others an understanding of our role in the evolutionary process. Third, he suggests we support a unified and self-actualized planetary society—that we seek forms of governance and economic systems that are more evolvable and better at organizing human cooperation.[19]

Kelly

For an interesting twist on the direction of evolution, let's consider the viewpoint of technology writer and philosopher Kevin Kelly in his provocatively titled book, *What Technology Wants*. Kelly points out that our evolutionary past has included major biological changes, where we moved from one replicating molecule through numerous stages that included the emergence of DNA, cells, sexual reproduction, more complex organisms, colonies, primates, and on up to language-based societies.

It is here that he believes that our future evolution may be moving over into the realm of technology. Kelly writes that the bulk of our recent human evolution has not been physical, but is shown in our products or artifacts. Hence, we see the emergence of language-based societies and technological growth via things such as our original oral traditions that evolved into writing, printing, books, scientific method, mass production, and industrial culture, leading up to today's ubiquitous global communication. In other words, humanity's evolution moved up a biological process to our current physical state and then jumped over to continue its future development in the realm of information and knowledge by way of the mechanism of technical advancements.

Much of Kelly's book offers support for his basic thesis. If we can accept that there is an evolutionary process at play in technological advances (and Kelly makes a good case for it), the next question is, "Where is the evolution of technology going?" That's another way of asking, "What is it that technology wants?" From his research, Kelly extrapolates a number of characteristics that are "desired" by technology, and they are basically what biological life also wants. His list includes thirteen trends that by now should sound familiar, including emergence, complexity, diversity, mutualism, and evolvability.

Several times we have heard the assertion that evolution is moving toward greater complexity. But what exactly is *complexity*? Not everyone agrees on its definition, but most definitions include the concept that something is considered to be more complex when both of the following are true: (1) It has more interdependent elements interacting in relationship with each other in a system, and (2) Those elements change based upon the feedback within the system.

In other words, greater complexity involves something that has more parts to it, and those parts are connected. As they interact in these connections, the interactions cause the parts themselves to evolve or change.

A human obviously is more complex than a single-cell organism. Human society is more complex than an individual human. The printing press is more complex than printing by hand. Publishing on the Internet is more complex than the printing press. The less complex something is, the better we can predict how it will work in a given situation. The more complex, the less we can guess how the system will act.

What does Kelly mean by *mutualism*? To him, the idea also could be referred to as *co-evolution*. The concept is that as life evolves, it creates increasing levels of dependency on other life. Sometimes this is just parasitic—the parasite lives off the efforts of the host, with the host receiving little or nothing in exchange. At higher levels, mutualism can lead to a symbiotic relationship where two species grow and change in response to one another. Kelly points out that as life continues to evolve, nature first creates more opportunities for dependencies among species, and later creates increased possibilities for cooperation among members of the same species. Kelly believes that our technological innovations (such as our ability to work together online and share information globally) are bringing an interesting blending of humanity and technology—the latter contributing to greater possibilities for cooperation between humans. Interestingly, Kelly also sees technology cooperating with technology for technology's evolution! Similarly, technology is supporting humanity's expansion of its ability to direct its own evolution (that is, its evolvability), as well as assisting technology's own evolvability.

Okay, but where is all this evolution going? According to Kelly, "Evolution, life, mind, and the *technium* [his coined word for all technology] are infinite games. Their game is to keep the game going... To explore every way to play the game, to include all games, all possible players, to widen what is meant by playing, to spend all, to hoard nothing, to see the universe with improbable plays, and if possible to surpass everything that has come before."

Kelly notes the similarity of his findings with those of futurist and self-acknowledged atheist Ray Kurzweil. In his book, *The Singularity Is Near*, Kurzweil wrote, "Evolution moves towards greater complexity, greater elegance, greater knowledge, greater intelligence, greater beauty, greater creativity, and greater levels of subtle attributes such as love. In every monotheistic tradition God is likewise described by all of these qualities only without limitation... So evolution moves inexorably toward this conception of God, although never quite reaching this ideal."[20]

Mystics

Let us turn from what technology wants and the predictions of an "atheist" to what might appear to be the polar opposite: the direction that some mystics say we are headed in.

But first, what exactly is a *mystic*? All the major religions have a mystical subset. For example, Zen is a mystical type of Buddhism. The Sufis are a mystical sect of Islam. The Kabbalah represents the mystical teachings of Judaism. Even Christianity has had its share of mystical teachers, such as Teresa of Ávila, Meister Eckhart, St. John of the Cross, and others.

The common denominator of all the mystical sects and teachers is their proclamation of their access to information beyond our normal existence. We might consider that they have a finely tuned intuitive sense. Frequently, we hear of mystics having visions (some might say "hallucinations") where they experience dimensions beyond our physically perceivable world. Simply stated, most mystics believe they have cultivated a personal relationship with God or the Divine.

Generally, the claim that one can talk to God is met with disbelief—if not a straitjacket! Yet, throughout the history of humanity, there have been individuals providing messages for the rest of us from their mystical state of knowing. In many cases, these individuals and their messages have stood the test of time. Something about what they said resonated with others, such that their teachings were able to propagate.

Let's consider what some mystics have offered regarding what they see as our evolutionary future.

Teilhard de Chardin

Pierre Teilhard de Chardin was a French Jesuit priest and paleontologist whose writings were banned by the Catholic Church until after his death in 1955. Described as a mystic and an evolutionary scientist, all the scientific studies he conducted validated for him the truth of evolution—a fact not well accepted by the Church during his lifetime. "Evolution," he wrote, "is no longer a hypothesis but a condition to which henceforth all hypotheses must conform."

Teilhard also wrote of his mystical experiences and what has been called "cosmic consciousness." He viewed both science and mystical ways of knowing as being valid. In fact, he stated that over time science would be progressively more "impregnated by mysticism"—not to direct it but to animate it.

In his book, *The Phenomenon of Man*, Teilhard wrote of the evolution of the universe and the Earth, from its primordial state through the development of humanity and beyond. One relevant concept he offered was that the Earth is entering a third major development in its history. It had moved through a period of the geosphere, where the planet was driven by inanimate objects, and then the biosphere, where life had been the major force. Now, he saw that we were moving into what he called the *noosphere*, a time when the interplay of all human minds will be a determining power in the planet's direction.

Teilhard saw these stages of Earth's development as having a purpose. Each stage was taking us to higher levels of complexity, as well as higher levels of consciousness—and, they were essential in moving the planet toward something he called "the Omega point." He saw the Omega point as a force that was drawing us toward it, as well as the direction we are headed in. He offered that this Omega point could be equated to the concept of "the Christ," a force and presence that is both within us and outside of us, drawing us together, reuniting us in our sense of oneness.

Teilhard described five attributes of this Omega point. One is that, even though it may be some future point we are collectively headed toward, it already exists. It is not something that will be coming into existence later. Two, the Omega point is not an abstract concept but rather a presence or "being" with whom we can sense a relationship. Three, there is a transcendent nature to the Omega point such that it not only exists outside of us, but ultimately, outside the bounds of the physical universe. Four, the point is autonomous, free from the limitations of space and time. Five, there is an irreversible aspect to it—it must happen; it is imperative that we move toward it. In a sense, one might consider the Omega point to be the Divine, Spirit, or God.

The force of love held an important role in our evolutionary path, according to Teilhard, who said, "Driven by the forces of love, the fragments of the world seek each other so that the world may come to being." He also affirmed, "Love is the affinity which links and draws together the elements of the world... Love, in fact, is the agent of universal synthesis."....and, "Someday, after mastering the winds, the waves, the tides and gravity, we shall harness for God the energies of love, and then, for a second time in the history of the world, man will have discovered fire." In other words, Teilhard is calling us to see love as an evolutionary force, one that is drawing us outside of ourselves and calling us to be reunited with all of life—the goal of our evolution[21].

Rumi

One of the most well-known mystics is the Sufi poet Rumi, who lived during the 1200s yet is one of the bestselling poets in modern times. There is something about his writings that has always resonated with people. Rumi clearly was an evolutionary.

Consider the following, from his Wikipedia article: "Rumi was an evolutionary thinker in the sense that he believed that the spirit after devolution from the divine Ego undergoes an evolutionary process by which it comes nearer and nearer to the same divine Ego. All matter in the universe obeys this law and this movement is due to an inbuilt urge (which Rumi calls 'love') to evolve and seek enjoinment with the divinity from which it has emerged. Evolution into a human being from an animal is only one stage in this process. The doctrine of the Fall of Adam is reinterpreted as the devolution of the Ego from the universal ground of divinity and is a universal, cosmic phenomenon. ... Rumi believes that there is a specific goal to the process: the attainment of God. For Rumi, God is the ground as well as the goal of all existence."[22]

From that perspective, read these lines from one of his poems:
> *I died as a mineral and became a plant,*
> *I died as plant and rose to animal,*
> *I died as animal and I was Man.*
> *Why should I fear? When was I less by dying?*
> *Yet once more I shall die as Man, to soar*
> *With angels bless'd; but even from angelhood*
> *I must pass on: all except God doth perish.*[23]

Meister Eckhart

Contemporary to the time of Rumi was the German Christian mystic, Meister Eckhart. Eckhart presented interesting spiritual concepts that led to him being tried as a heretic by the Catholic Church. Of note was his idea that God, out of its overabundance of love, gave birth to the "Son" and that the "Word" was instilled in all of its creation. That is, everyone has a divine aspect that is imbedded in each of us and was placed there by the outpouring of God's love for us. Yet, at the same time, God is calling us back to itself. [24]

Here are a few lines from the book, *Meditations by Meister Eckhart*, that convey this point:

> *The divine countenance*
> *is capable of maddening and driving*
> *all souls out of their senses*
> *with longing for it.*

> *When it does this by its very divine nature*
> *it is thereby*
> *drawing all things to itself.*
>
> *Every creature –*
> *whether it knows it or not –*
> *seeks repose.*[25]

Gnostics

Going back even farther in time to the Gnostics, we find similar revelations. The Gnostics were a Christian sect that arose in the first few centuries of the Common Era. They had their own gospels, which were widely circulated and read before the currently known canonical books of the Bible were established. Many scholars believe that the decision made by the men in attendance at the First Council of Nicaea in 325 CE to proclaim that Jesus was the son of God, and that his divinity was unique to him (that is, in effect, saying that God was not in others) led to many seeing the Gnostic gospels as heretical. Hence, the gospels were banned and burned, and generally were known for many years only by way of their critics, who referenced and quoted them in their writings. Only in recent years were copies of many of these early Christian gospels discovered.

Central to the Gnostic teachings was the idea that each of us could develop our own relationship with God. In these teachings, personal "knowing" of God is essential. The physical world is seen as coming from the divine world, albeit as a copy of a "lower" quality or essence. The divine "fell" into the world and into each of us. Through a process of "awakening," we are called to return to our divine state. It is through our direct experience of the divine that we make this "return." Of course, the direct experience of the divine is the key component of the mystical experience![26]

One of the better-known Gnostic gospels that recently was discovered is the Gospel of Thomas. Here are a couple of quotes from it, which are relevant to our discussion:

"Whoever drinks from my mouth will become as I am; I myself shall become that person, and the hidden things will be revealed to him." (Thomas 108)

"...the Kingdom of God is inside of you, and it is outside of you. When you come to know yourselves, then you will become known, and you will realize that it is you who are the sons of the living Father. But if you will not know yourselves, you dwell in poverty, and it is you who are that poverty." (Thomas 3)

Both of these quotes point toward an evolutionary process of self-discovery. We are called to look within, and when we do, we discover our truth, that we are connected to all, to God.

Bruteau

It is not just mystics from the near and distant past who point us toward an evolutionary reconnecting with our divine source. A more recent such contemplative is Beatrice Bruteau, author of numerous books including *God's Ecstasy: the Creation of a Self-Creating World*. In a recent interview with *EnlightenNext* magazine, she describes the interaction of evolution and God: "A theology of evolution sees God as deeply involved in the evolutionary process of the world. God is making the world by means of evolution. And the evolutionary process in its turn is seen as striving toward God. So, you see, God is Self-expressing and Self-realizing in evolution."

In Bruteau's view, there is a basic urgency with all of us—within all of life—to grow and evolve. This plays out in the smallest forms of life and in our lives. Evolution brings greater complexity and an increase in consciousness. Creative unions are formed, where we begin to see the interplay of all of life. Past evolution has occurred due to random events, but we have reached a point where we are aware of the evolutionary process and the role we play within it. According to Bruteau, "The individual human being can, and we, by our concerted intention, can make something that hasn't existed before."[27]

Conclusion

We've looked at several sources I've chosen in hopes that you will begin to see some common themes about the possibilities of our evolutionary future. Obviously, there are sources I could have drawn upon that were not in alignment with the ones I presented; I also I could have presented more that were. At this point, let's see what commonalities may have emerged.

Common Themes

Here is what I culled from these mystics, scientists, and philosophers regarding some common themes about the direction of our evolution:

- Greater complexity in all our systems
- Greater ability to consciously control the evolutionary process
- Less focus on deficiency (basic) needs, more focus on higher needs
- Less focus on material needs, greater focus on spiritual needs
- Greater levels of cooperation among people
- Greater knowledge transferred to the next generation via learning
- Expanding technical accomplishments
- A melding of science and spirituality
- Increased emphasis on living life's calling or purpose
- Greater levels of human service to one another
- Expanding power of love leading us to feel a greater sense of interconnectedness
- Greater degree of our sense of oneness

Did you identify some other themes? If so, how do they fit into the above list and into your view of where we may collectively be headed?

Ultimately the question becomes, "How do we move in that direction?" Again, it's up to each of us, in our thoughts and actions and in the choices we make. As you hold this list in mind, let's take it from the abstract to the concrete. The above-listed possible characteristics of our evolutionary future don't necessarily paint a vivid picture of a future that we can focus our intentions upon. Let's move to some possibilities that we might view as a true "vision" we can focus on with our collective power.

A Compelling Common Vision?

In this chapter, we move into exploring what might be a personal vision for you and me that could lead us toward focusing the power of our intentions. Then, we consider if there have been any collective efforts to create a common set of intentions that we might rally around. It turns out that there is at least one good possibility for us to consider.

Getting Real

But first, let's address the elephant in the room: *How realistic is this?*

Can we truly create a world that works for everyone? I am an optimist but also a realist. I believe we can bring about a future where everyone is valued and has an opportunity for success. I believe we can bring about a future where everyone has their basic needs met and has the opportunity to work on higher growth needs. It's not going to be easy, but it can be done.

The current challenges facing humanity discussed throughout this book were key forces leading me to write it. I have concerns for the world that my children and future generations are inheriting. I want to leave the world a better place for them, and I hope you want to leave the world a better place for those you care about.

I want you to feel empowered. I want you to know that you have the tools and the ability to truly be yourself—to live the life you came here to live. I want this for you because I realize that the more you and I become our true selves, the more we become in service to humanity and create a world that works for everyone.

So, if we are all alike and share so much, can we also remember that we share a common evolutionary path? I recognize that our human minds want to take the concept of the direction of our evolutionary future and put it in concrete terms. What can I do right now to move us to that positive future?

Ultimately I must ask the questions: Where do I want humanity to go? What does a positive future really look like? What does it mean to create a world that works for everyone? What does that look like for the world? What do we need to do to move to that vision?

In contemplating these questions, we begin to realize there is a gap between where we are and that idealistic future. Our realistic side calls us to ask how can we move to a world where we cooperate with one another and help others to meet their needs, when our basic human nature is one of competition and survival of the fittest? If one of us tries to jumpstart the "love train" of cooperation, won't they just be the "weakest link" and get devoured by all those stronger people? Maybe, maybe not.

The fact is that as long as we have planetary conditions where people live with shortage and lack, they always will be motivated by their deficiencies. If their conditions could be improved so that all their basic needs were met, they would have a better chance of moving into higher motivations where they would seek to live a self-actualizing life. Could it be that our cooperative future is connected to ensuring that everyone's basic needs are met?

In the theory of Spiral Dynamics, everyone is born into the lower worldviews and must move through different stages of varying life conditions before they can reach the higher levels. They cannot bypass developmental stages.

Someone living in an advanced society where basic needs are met and an excellent education is provided, where those around them are expressing higher consciousness (seeing the interconnectedness of everything and everyone) has an excellent chance of moving into that awareness as they grow up. However, someone born into a tribal society where there is a sense of poverty, people struggle to meet basic needs, there is little or no education, and it is obvious that the person or group in power lives well while others struggle—a child born under these conditions has little hope of developing this expanded vision of cooperation. It simply is not something they can relate to; their life is about fighting to survive. Perhaps our cooperative future is connected to up lifting all societies to these higher stages of development.

When we have expanded our care and concern for others and assumed this evolutionary viewpoint, somewhere within each of us, we can't help but realize that our positive future—one that avoids any kind of doomsday scenario—is tied to everyone else on the planet and their success. Competition and fighting over wealth and resources takes us to a negative future. Cooperation, love, and sharing resources takes us to a positive future. Those of us that are aware of this fork in the road must choose to take action to increase the standard of living for everyone. Doing so is our best chance for each pocket of consciousness on this planet to evolve to its highest level. Ultimately, there is a high dose of "reality" in seeking a common vision.

One Possible Personal Vision

This brings us back to our vision. What is your vision for a world that works for everyone? My personal vision, which I suspect would look a lot like most people's vision, incorporates the following elements:

- I have all of my basic physical needs easily met.
- I have good health.
- I have a nice home that protects me from the elements.
- I live in a society that assures me basic freedoms and safety.
- I have a good education and opportunity to grow.
- I have a network of friends and family who love me.
- have the opportunity to grow my standard of living to a comfortable level.
- I have the opportunity to express my creative abilities.
- I have the opportunity to develop my spiritual nature.
- I answer my calling to be of service to others.

If I were to use my personal collective vision to create one for all of humanity, it would essentially read the same! The word "I" would be replaced with "we," and the word "my" would be replaced with "our." It would look like this:

- We have all of our basic physical needs easily met.
- We have good health.
- We have a nice home that protects us from the elements.
- We live in a society that assures our basic freedoms and safety.
- We have a good education and opportunity to grow.

- We have a network of friends and family who love us.
- We have the opportunity to grow our standard of living to a comfortable level.
- We have the opportunity to express our creative abilities.
- We have the opportunity to develop our spiritual nature.
- We answer our calling to be of service to others.

Doesn't that sound nice? The interesting thing is that at some point as our consciousness expands, we begin to realize that what we want for ourselves is what others want, and it becomes what we want for them. The Golden Rule really comes alive!

It's one thing for me to have a vision for all of humanity, but what if it isn't a shared vision? Is there not more power if we all hold a vision of our highest future, on which we can focus our attention and actions? Obviously that is true. Is there such a vision around which we can all rally?

Uniting Nations with a Common Vision

Wouldn't it be wonderful if we could pull together the entire planet and create a vision statement that we all agreed upon and gained commitment to pursue? Of course, our cynical side may suggest that we would never get everyone to agree on one vision. Maybe that's true. But my optimistic side believes that the vast majority of us would agree on certain key aspects of that vision. And, I'll bet it would include a lot of those characteristics we just listed.

We may not be able to assemble everybody on the planet to brainstorm and write words on flip charts, but do we have anything already created that points us to an example of a potential, optimistic future? Let's consider a few possibilities.

What about the United States (US)? The US does not have a formal vision statement, although Wikipedia's article on mission statements points to the preamble to the US constitution as being a perfect example of one: "We the People of the United States, in Order to form a more perfect Union, establish Justice, insure domestic Tranquility, provide for the common defense, promote the general Welfare, and secure the Blessings of Liberty to ourselves and our Posterity, do ordain and establish this Constitution for the United States of America." This statement outlines the purpose behind the creation (and ongoing actions) of the US government. Yet, regarding a common statement detailing where the American people are headed collectively, neither the preamble statement nor any other that I can find outlines such a path. One might consider that the United States could benefit from a common vision!

What about the United Nations (UN)? The UN spells out what could be considered a mission and vision statement in the preamble to its charter. Here is the beginning, which might be considered its "mission":

"We the peoples of the United Nations determined: to save succeeding generations from the scourge of war, which twice in our lifetime has brought untold sorrow to mankind, and; to reaffirm faith in fundamental human rights, in the dignity and worth of the human person, in the equal rights of men and women and of nations large and small, and; to establish conditions under which justice and respect for the obligations arising from treaties and other sources of international law can be maintained, and to promote social progress and better standards of life in larger freedom..."

And then come the following words, which might be seen as the UN's vision statement:

"And for these ends: to practice tolerance and live together in peace with one another as good neighbours, and; to unite our strength to maintain international peace and security, and; to ensure, by the acceptance of principles and the institution of methods, that armed force shall not be used, save in the common interest, and; to employ international machinery for the promotion of the economic and social advancement of all peoples, have resolved to combine our efforts to accomplish these aims."

We could consider that the essence of this vision statement is to work toward a peaceful world where all people have opportunities for economic and social advancement. Elsewhere I have read that the UN's vision statement is simply the word "peace." Either way, these words give us a noble statement and cause, although it might be beneficial for the UN to create a more specific and inspiring future vision. In my opinion, we could use a more compelling vision.

In September 2000, the UN adopted a "Millennium Declaration" that comes close to painting a vision that might inspire us all. This document was created, as it says in its first few lines, "at the dawn of a new millennium, to reaffirm our faith in the Organization and its Charter as indispensable foundations of a more peaceful, prosperous and just world."

The nine-page document goes on to outline specific values and actions that the UN sees as important for the twenty-first century. Let's examine a few concepts from the Millennium Declaration, starting with the "values" that are

set out in the document:
- **Freedom**. Men and women have the right to live their lives and raise their children in dignity, free from hunger and from the fear of violence, oppression, or injustice. Democratic and participatory governance based on the will of the people best assures these rights.
- **Equality**. No individual and no nation must be denied the opportunity to benefit from development. The equal rights and opportunities of women and men must be assured.
- **Solidarity**. Global challenges must be managed in a way that distributes the costs and burdens fairly in accordance with basic principles of equity and social justice. Those that suffer or benefit the least deserve help from those that benefit the most.
- **Tolerance**. Human beings must respect one other, in all their diversity of belief, culture, and language. Differences within and between societies should neither be feared nor repressed, but cherished as a precious asset of humanity. A culture of peace and dialogue among all civilizations should be actively promoted.
- **Respect for nature**. Prudence must be shown in the management of all living species and natural resources, in accordance with the precepts of sustainable development. Only in this way can the immeasurable riches provided to us by nature be preserved and passed on to our descendants. The current unsustainable patterns of production and consumption must be changed in the interest of our future welfare and that of our descendants.
- **Shared responsibility**. Responsibility for managing worldwide economic and social development, as

well as threats to international peace and security, must be shared among the nations of the world and should be exercised multilaterally. As the most universal and most representative organization in the world, the UN must play the central role.

This document paints a picture of a world where there is a movement up the "needs" levels and where everyone plays a part in the development of "the all," while still retaining personal rights and responsibilities. I see a healthy balance that includes meeting the needs of autonomy, mastery, and purpose that Daniel Pink described, as well as ensuring that there is a mechanism for uplifting those who may not currently have similar opportunities. In addition, this vision includes most, if not all, of the characteristics we listed in our vision!

The specific actions outlined by the UN document fall into the following categories: (1) Peace, security, and disarmament; (2) Development and poverty eradication; (3) Protecting our common environment; (4) Human rights, democracy, and good governance; (5) Protecting the vulnerable; (6) Meeting the special needs of Africa; and (7) Strengthening the UN.

Even without probing into the specifics, we can see that there is a higher-consciousness effort to ensure that we are collectively working to meet basic human needs. However, here is one that goes right to the heart of this intention: "We will spare no effort to free our fellow men, women and children from the abject and dehumanizing conditions of extreme poverty, to which more than a billion of them are currently subjected. We are committed to making the right to development a reality for everyone and to freeing the entire human race from want."

Think about this: If we "free the entire human race

from want," they are able to move to addressing higher needs. And, although that can lead them to increasing the desire for more consumer goods, which can tax the planet's resources, that "acquisition of stuff" phase of human development is a natural step on the evolutionary path. If we truly desire to grow into the place where all humans are motivated by higher self-actualization needs and from higher worldviews, then all humans need to have the life conditions to evolve to those levels.

I encourage you to read the full document that I have included in the Appendix. Parts of it are truly inspirational.

But what about taking this vision to the next step—intentions and actions? This declaration statement led to the creation of UN Millennium Goals, a set of key benchmarks seen as important for bringing about a peaceful, prosperous, and just world. In a manner of speaking, the UN Millennium Goals are the specific intentions that came from the vision of the UN Millennium Declaration.

These kinds of big, inspiring goals are what business author Jim Collins calls "big hairy audacious goals" (BHAGs) in his book, *Built to Last*."[28]. His point was that enduring companies inspire their employees to buy into their vision statements by way of BHAGs—something that is specific and actionable, but is a stretch. If you lend your energy to its accomplishment, you know that you have contributed in some way to improving life. The BHAG makes the flowery language of the vision statement come alive. If it can work for great companies, then it can work for great planets. I want to live on a great planet.

Following are the eight UN Millennium Goals:

- Eradicate extreme poverty and hunger.
- Achieve universal primary education.
- Promote gender equality and empower women.
- Reduce child mortality rates.
- Improve maternal health.
- Combat HIV/AIDS, malaria, and other diseases.
- Ensure environmental sustainability.
- Develop a global partnership for development.

Each of these goals has specific targets with measurable yardsticks to determine if we are making progress. For example, under the first goal is the following target: "Halve the proportion of people living on less than $1 a day." From these goals (or intentions), the UN and its member countries and partner non-governmental organizations have been taking specific actions. I encourage you to read more about the goals and actions on the Internet[29].

The optimistic point is that humanity is making great strides toward the Millennium Goals. A recent report by the World Bank shows that "two-thirds of developing countries are on track or close to meeting the Millennium Development Goals."[30] It appears that we are well on the way to more than halving the number of people living on $1 per day. Recent data shows great strides in the availability of educational opportunities, with especially strong growth in schooling for women. A recent cover story of the *Christian Science Monitor* in late 2011 reported that, in spite of what we see in the news, there are good stories all around us. The magazine listed four positive trends: (1) war and violence have decreased; (2) the number of countries governed by democracy has increased; (3) world poverty has decreased; and (4) the gender-based wage gap between men and women is shrinking.[31]

These are great indicators of the progress we can make for all of humanity when we focus our collective selves toward a goal. They also give us something we can focus on with gratitude: that we are making headway in growing our world toward one that works for everyone. Yet, even with the progress, there are still tremendous opportunities for improvement. Meeting the goal to reduce extreme poverty by 2015 still leaves over 880 million people living on less than $1 per day. Perhaps it's time to set a new goal.

Did you find something here that you can visualize? As the second key to moving us across that bridge to our highest future, I encourage you to develop your own vision of that future based on what you have read here, adding your own unique perspective. Then review it, share it, and live as if it were true.

Part Four:

Becoming Yourself

In the fourth section of the book, we will explore the following ideas:

- The third key to crossing the bridge to our highest future is *becoming yourself*.
- Becoming yourself is not about being selfish.
- Becoming yourself is about identifying your life's true calling and then living fully.
- There are ways to identify your life's true calling.
- You need to let go of any limitations or excuses that keep you from believing you can live the life you were meant to live.
- As you take the seemingly selfish action to become yourself, you ultimately are giving your gift to others, and your selfish act becomes a selfless act.

Identifying and Answering Your Calling

The essential message I hope you get from this book is to *be yourself*. You may wonder, what exactly do I mean by that?

No doubt some will hear those words as a call to live a narcissistic life—to look at the world as your oyster, there for your taking. It's all about you! Live your life in hedonistic overdrive, fulfilling your senses, gathering possessions, and grabbing what you want without concern for others. Let me be very clear—this is *not* what I mean by "being yourself"!

A person can get stuck in narcissistic selfishness at any of the worldview levels. Let's consider each.

Narcissism at the traditional level is expressed by a person that doesn't care about what others think or feel. It includes a selfish desire to impose one's beliefs and values on others because "you know better" or have "higher morals." The cultural battles fought by traditionalists seeking to impose a complete ban on abortions, advocating abstinence, restricting access to contraceptives, preventing the teaching of evolution theories, and so on is indicative of a selfish lack of concern for what others think or want. This is not to say that everyone who is favor of these things is exhibiting narcissistic selfishness, but if their underlying intention is to impose their beliefs on others, they need to take a long look at those intentions.

Narcissism at the material level is expressed by a person that wants to gather wealth and possessions at the expense of others. That aspect of Wall Street in the financial crisis of 2008 revealed a number of people that were willing to do anything for their own material gain, no matter what harm it caused to others. Similarly, the trend toward increasing corporate political power to ensure that government decisions support corporations in gathering even more wealth at the expense of the average person is indicative of a selfish narcissism. Individuals who don't care about the welfare of other humans and are concerned only with amassing more material wealth need to take a clear look at their intentions.

Narcissism also can show up at the materialist worldview level as a militant form of atheism that seeks to put down those who "don't believe in rationalism and science." Similar to traditionalists (although most materialists would be shocked at the comparison), they have the sense that their values are better than everyone else's. They view themselves as smarter and better educated. Anyone who doesn't believe that every answer can be found in material science and rational thought is a small-minded individual stuck in old myths or seduced by "New Age" thinking.

Narcissism at the humanistic level can show up in a number of ways as well. First, it can be expressed in a "caretaker" mentality that the person or group is here to "save the world" or "save others." Welfare or humanitarian aid that is intended only to take care of other individuals and keep them in a state of perpetual subservient need (such that they must be "taken care of" by the more fortunate people) is indicative of this narcissism. Secondly, narcissism at the humanistic level can show as a selfish focus on one's own personal development at the expense of those around us, who may need something from us. Ignoring the needs of friends, family, a partner, or society while we attend

Part Four: Becoming Yourself

one more self-help workshop can be viewed as selfish behavior.

Finally, as with the other worldviews, if we think that our viewpoint is the only "smart" one, that opinion is also narcissism. Just as materialists view themselves as smarter than traditionalists, humanists can be seduced into believing they are "smarter" or "higher" in some hierarchy of understanding. It is one thing to be aware that there are natural hierarchies in life, and quite another to use that awareness as a means of putting down others who don't think as you do.

Let me repeat—narcissistic selfishness is *not* "being yourself"!

As I see it, being yourself means that you answer the call to live your life purpose. Being yourself means living the life you were placed on Earth to live. It means recognizing the unique gifts you have to give to the world, and then moving forward to express them regardless of the barriers you meet.

Do you really believe your life has a purpose? Do you believe there is a reason you came to Earth at the time and place you did and then moved through your unique life experiences? Do you believe you were given a special talent or gift to express in and through your life?

I obviously believe we do, or I wouldn't be encouraging you to live your life purpose!

I recognize that some of you reading these words might not believe that any of our lives have purpose. Some of you may believe your existence is simply a random event based on purely materialistic factors. In this view, physical evolution gave rise through mutation and survival of the fittest to the animal we call humans. The development of consciousness and the sense of a personal self are either a random byproduct of our physical evolution, or these uniquely human characteristics gave us some evolutionary advantage. Either way, you might think, it's all devoid of meaning. Our attempts to find meaning in life and a purpose for our life are may be just some strange, evolutionary quirk in our brains. We are being tricked into thinking we have a purpose.

If you want to believe that, it's okay with me. My personal belief is that individuals who have such a nihilistic view of life hold that viewpoint because it's in alignment with a strict materialistic worldview. A person with this outlook must see life as a bunch of random physical things knocking around into one another. The only meaning one might get from such a worldview is that your purpose is to develop your skills so as to manipulate the world and gather all the physical possessions you can. In any case, this view of life is rather depressing to me. I believe that life holds more meaning.

My life experience has led me to realize that all of us are here for some special reason. We are here to move through life experiences, good and bad, to learn lessons and to develop and grow. We are here to evolve, to gain new perspectives, and to see greater meaning. As a part of this developmental process, I believe strongly that each person was given a unique task to perform during this lifetime. This task involves learning and expressing some distinctive ability. The special capacity may be similar to that of some other humans, but your special way of showing up in life and utilizing this ability is subtly different from any one else's.

This calling, ability, or talent can be seen in general as either very rare or very common. People tend to place value judgments upon them. It's easy to spot the rare talents. With artists and musicians, writers, high-performing athletes, and others that are called to the spotlight and honored for their celebrity, it's easy to see that they are expressing themselves and living their calling. It may not be so easy to spot others who are doing the same, outside the glare of celebrity. You may be called to be yourself by way of being a parent, working in a store, digging ditches, gardening or farming, sewing clothes, programming computers, or a myriad of other endeavors. Being yourself is not about being rich or famous. Being yourself is about identifying your true talent and then living your life expressing that talent—no matter what it is.

Doing this has a number of advantages: Your life is more joyful. Events flow in a more synchronistic manner, with things lining up for you in just the right way at just the right time. Work truly becomes, as Kahlil Gibran called it, "love in action"—something that fills your life with pleasure. You shift your focus from believing you lack something to knowing you have everything you need.

In addition, an extremely beneficial aspect of being yourself, of living your life's calling, is that you let go of feeling that you are in competition with others and move to a place of wanting to cooperate with them. You shift to the motivation of being in service to humanity. Humanity's challenges could be easily overcome if all of us truly became ourselves.

The truth is, each of us has a purpose for being here—we all have a special talent or ability, and life will conspire to make sure we use it. One of the areas I described that we all have in common is our desire to *make a difference*. We all have a calling.

This book represents me living my calling—though it, I am "calling you" as well. I am calling you to shift your attention away from any current focus on our differences and to move to seeing how we are united. I am calling you to expand your care and concern for more people. I am calling you to develop an evolutionary way of looking at life. And, in all of this, I am ultimately calling you to answer your inner calling and live your purpose as well.

It has become increasingly clear to me that when any of us answers our personal calling to live our life's purpose, doing so brings us true happiness and joy. In finding that joy, we ultimately shift into becoming a personal vessel in service to all humanity. It's a beautiful thing to see unfold.

"Many persons have a wrong idea of what constitutes true happiness. It is not attained through self-gratification but through fidelity to a worthy purpose," stated Helen Keller.

As the Dali Lama said, "Our prime purpose in this life is to help others."

What is your vision for your life, if you are living on purpose? What is your passion? Maybe you already know. If so, you can skim through the next section and jump ahead to living your passion.

If you're not sure or truly don't know what is your life purpose, then the question becomes, "What is a *true calling*?" I can't answer that specifically for you, but I can direct you to guidance that is available within yourself. Let's look at several ways you might answer the question for yourself. These include studying your life's patterns, listening to your intuition, asking yourself some critical questions, and using a self-discovery exercise to get in touch with your true passions.

Studying Life's Patterns

If we are not living our passion, our outer lives may keep

recreating experiences to redirect us back to it. Over and over we find similar patterns out-picturing. Coincidences occur; the same challenges pop up. Often, if we would just step back and look at our life from a higher vantage point, we could see the patterns.

Here's a quick exercise that will allow you to do just that.

Take a large piece of paper and draw a horizontal line across it. This represents the timeline of your life. At the end of the line on the left side, write the words "my birth." At the end of the line on the right side, write the words "present day." On the space on the timeline between your birth and now, label the appropriate points of time and any necessary descriptive words in response to these suggestions. On the timeline, indicate the following:

- The major crossroads in your life when you made a choice that moved you in a new direction.

- The major roads not taken in your life—that is, the points when you could have made a major choice but you stayed in place.

- The major crises that have occurred in your life (whatever a "crisis" may be to you). Label what you learned from each crisis.

- Indicate the major successes that have occurred in your life. Label what you gained from each success.

- List any major milestones in your life that are not already listed. Label what you gained from each milestone.

Now take a moment and look at your timeline. Do you see any trends, any messages? Has your life been redirecting you to similar kinds of experiences or learning? What does any of this have to say about the purpose of your life?

Listening to Your Intuition

It's my belief that each of us has an inner wisdom we can tap whenever we want guidance. The steps to do so are simple.

First, consider the question, "What is my purpose for this lifetime?" (The wording is not important; if you have a question that resonates better with you, use it.)

Second, while holding that question in mind, sit quietly in silence. Be open to any guidance that comes forth. As thoughts flow through your awareness, simply notice them. Don't dwell on any thoughts or subjects; simply note the content in your mind and return to being open with the question.

Third, as you come out of the silence, take a piece of paper or journal and write about the thoughts that came flowing by you. If, in writing about the thoughts you experienced, new thoughts come forth, write them down too. Simply allow your words to flow on the paper. Don't judge where the thoughts or words come from; simply allow them to flow.

When you are done, look for any trends or messages. Tapping this inner guidance takes practice and should be repeated a number of times until you feel comfortable with it. However, know that you can always access this inner awareness.

Questioning Yourself

Beyond looking outside of your life for patterns, or going inside for guidance, you can bring the two ways of *knowing* together in a process of asking yourself directed questions. Following is a list of some questions that might guide you in discovering your purpose.

Again, I would suggest that you take some quiet time to reflect upon and journal your thoughts to these specific questions:

- What do you think is the one problem you were born to understand?
- Write down a subject that you can speak about with genuine authority, as you have lived through it.
- What section of the bookstore do you visit first or spend the most time in?
- Picture yourself at a crossroads where you can see a signpost up ahead with two signs pointing in different directions. What words are written on those signs? Which one do you feel an inner pull toward, even if it doesn't make logical sense?
- What are the most natural abilities you have always displayed?
- What is something people have been telling about yourself, throughout your whole life?
- If you didn't have to worry about consequences, what one act of chaos would you introduce into your life right now?
- If someone said, "Just go for it"—what is "it"?
- If you were to write a book, what would it be about?
- If you could get the whole world's attention for thirty minutes, what would you talk about?
- When you contemplate your death, what do you think of that you haven't done yet that you need to do?
- What is your personal "divine urge" calling you to do?
- What is the next step in your evolution?

- What are you going to do, after reading this book, to take that step?

You probably can come up with similar questions. The key is to use these questions and your reflections to identify your true purpose in this lifetime. Stay with it until you know!

Discovering Your Passions

Following is an exercise that will help you discover your gifts, passions, and life purpose. Do the exercise for one week (seven consecutive days, starting on any day). Here are the steps:

1. Each day, record (on paper or electronically) everything you do or experience that brings you joy or fulfillment. Whenever you notice yourself feeling joy, write down what you were doing. It could be brushing your dog, having a cup of coffee, making a salad, debugging software, counseling someone, helping your neighbor fix his car, or watching a film. It doesn't have to be an obviously "productive" action, just something you enjoy. If you recall having already recorded an item on an earlier day, you don't have to repeat it, but if in doubt, write it down.

2. At the end of the week, review your daily lists to notice common themes. The possibilities for "themes" are unlimited. Here are some examples to get you started:

    a. Physically taking care of people, animals, plants, or human-made objects such as cars or homes

    b. Creating aesthetic beauty

    c. Repairing, restoring, or improving things

    d. Cleaning up (eliminating the unnecessary)

    e. Handling crises

    f. Offering compassion, counsel, and connection

    g. Teaching (sharing knowledge in a beneficial way)

    h. Investigating

    i. Transporting things

    j. Expressing creativity artistically in music, visual art, cooking, decorating, and other ways

    k. Inventing (this may be a computer program, mechanical device, or emotional-healing method)

    l. Creating structures (which may be a physical building or an organization)

3. Consolidate and organize the items on your list, grouping them by theme.

4. Review the themes and note ways you can combine them into "real-world" endeavors. Be imaginative and creative. For instance, you may have discovered that you really enjoy brewing a perfect cup of gourmet coffee and also love grooming and playing with your German shepherd. The two activities don't seem to be connected, but they can be—how about opening a dog-grooming salon that also is a gourmet coffee shop?

5. Look for ways you can express these themes in your life presently. Perhaps you love to clear out unnecessary stuff, but your home is already

uncluttered. However, you have a packrat friend who has indicated that he'd love to have help in clearing out his garage. You probably won't choose to turn every endeavor into a business, but you can trade services or just try something out to see if you want to take it farther. Another example: You love to sing and play guitar, and have been expressing this gift only by yourself and at family get-togethers. Check out opportunities for open-mic nights at local bars and restaurants.

Bringing Them All Together

After studying your life's patterns, checking in with your intuition and journaling, reflecting upon some key questions, or practicing the self-discovery exercise, you should begin to notice some common factors. Take some time to sit and reflect upon these common themes. At some point, I guarantee that you will start to have a good sense of what your life is about.

Complete the following sentence:

"The reason I came to earth at this time and place as this person is so that I could..."

"Thanks to Gregg Levoy for some of the questions presented in 'Questioning Yourself' and to Alexi Paulina for the ideas in 'Discovering Your Passions'."

Letting Go of Limitations

Hopefully, by now you have a general sense of your life purpose. I suspect you also have some internal dialogue in which some part of you is arguing that there is no way you can realistically live your life by following this identified purpose. Some part of you is saying, "That's all well and good, but you don't really think you could live your life by doing the thing you identified that you are supposed to do—*do you?*"

I'm calling you to overcome all the obstructions that present themselves to you in an attempt to deter you from your heart's path. What are some of these blocks and internal arguments? Here are a few common ones:

- You've gone through the exercises and are just not clear about your life's purpose.
- You don't see how you can make a living by following your heart.
- It will change your standard of living—you can't live on less money.
- Your parents want you to do something else.
- You're afraid you'll be judged negatively by others.
- You've invested a great deal of your life (schooling, years in your current career, and so forth) in another path.
- You are not worthy of it.
- It seems crazy, and others will think you're crazy.
- You won't fit in with society.

- You're not quite sure how to bring it about.
- It will change your relationships with friends and family.

These are some of the most common obstacles that arise; you likely have your own reasons for why you can't follow your purpose. I could list more, but I think you get the point.

What I want you to see is that *the only barriers that truly exist are in our own minds.* Neither society in general, nor any other people specifically, keep us from truly being ourselves. We think the limits are "out there," but *that thought* is really the limit.

I know some of you will hear that and immediately come up with a list of reasons related to forces "out there" that somehow place limits on you. Can we be limited by the physical characteristics we inherited? Can we be limited by our education? Can we be limited by the culture we were born into? Can we have restrictions placed upon us by institutions, governments, and people with power?

Yes, it's true that real or imagined external factors can make it harder to be our true self. But *harder* doesn't mean *impossible*. No matter what the outside forces are that may appear to be restricting, you always have the choice of how you respond to them.

I remember a number of years ago when I worked for the government and had been moving up the career ladder through various management or leadership positions. I had worked my way up to the "number two" job within my office. My sights were set on the top job. There were no guarantees I would get it, as occasionally political factors led to some placements that were given priority over career employees' advancement.

Eventually my boss retired. I assumed that I would be given the position on a temporary basis while agency leadership went through the process of announcing and filling the position permanently. It was customary for the number-two person to be placed in this "acting" capacity.

Unfortunately, that was not the case with me. Someone from outside the office was brought in to temporarily direct it. The snub immediately led me to believe that outside political forces were eliminating me from consideration for the job altogether. In that moment, I gave those external forces power over me.

This rejection led me to a lot of soul-searching and meditation. Ultimately, I realized that the "powers that be" held no true control over me. I still had the ability to choose my reaction to this situation. I still had the ability to release any attachment I had to getting the job. I still had the ability to work within my sphere of influence, no matter what job I had, for the betterment of myself and others.

It was from this place of personal power that I saw the gift I had been given: The gift to release attachments, the gift to choose my own reaction, and the gift to be in service.

As my new, temporary boss arrived, I had chosen to befriend him and support him in his success in the position. I knew that the more successful he was, the more successful our agency would be in fulfilling its mission and making a positive difference in the lives of our constituents. I guided my new leader through the intricacies of running the office and being effective in his relationships with local political types with whom he needed to interact. I prepared him and supported him fully.

Not long after he arrived and started receiving support from me, this individual shared that he had no interest in holding that job permanently. In fact, he felt the best thing he could do during his time in the position was to assist me in getting it myself. He began coaching me on aspects of our agency where he had more experience. This man gave me a tremendous gift, which led to my being selected for the job I desired.

This is just one example of many I could share, in which shifting my awareness from seeing myself as a victim to external powers toward claiming my power of choice led me to growth and advantageous outcomes. You probably have similar stories. Being yourself is always about claiming your power.

Do you really have the power to change these old belief systems? I believe you do.

So, what can you do to overcome the internal limitations you've placed upon yourself? The simple answer is to change your thinking. We've all heard the adage, "Change your thinking; change your life." That really is the answer! The answer may be simple, but no one said that changing your thinking is *easy*.

The goal is to reprogram yourself to let go of old, limiting beliefs and replace them with new, empowering ones. However, before getting to a three-step process on reprogramming your beliefs, let's look a bit more at one of the key reasons we often don't live life from what we think is our real true self—love, or more specifically, the lack of it.

The Human Dilemma of Love

Here's the dilemma, simply stated: We were born with a need for love, but most of us did not receive the unconditional love we needed as a child. We internalized this denial of love into a belief that we are not worthy of love (or of being our true self); and since then we have been seeking (perhaps without consciously being aware of it) the unconditional love we were denied. In many cases, the things we chase may not appear to be "love"; they may come in the form of substitutes---addictions, material wealth, power, and the like. In many cases, we hold back from showing others who we really are in our authentic nature because we think it is not good enough. We believe we are unworthy and if others knew or saw who we really were, they would see our "inferior nature."

Think back to my story of Lolete. In my memory, she gave me unconditional love. My parents truly loved me—I have no doubt of that, but they inadvertently gave me conditional love. I received love under the condition that I acted and believed as they wanted me to. When we left Lolete, I got the double whammy of losing the person who gave me unconditional love, as well receiving a message from my parents that something was wrong with me for grieving. On some level, I perceived a loss of their love as well.

There are a few things I want to highlight in telling my story. First, none of this was in my conscious awareness until many years later, when I was an adult. It was only in trying to truly understand myself that this realization came. Clarity around what I am presenting here came only through "processing" this information many times over many years.

Secondly, there is no blame to place anywhere in this story. Everyone did the best they could with the training and understanding of life that they had. My parents parented me with the skills they had learned from their parents; they loved me in the way they knew how. I love my parents, and the realization of how I internalized this event has nothing to do with that fact.

Thirdly, although I am presenting this "event" as a critical juncture in my personal development, (specifically, how I came to feel unlovable and unworthy), I know there were many events and factors that led me to question my self-worth.

That said, I think it is important for us all to realize there is a high likelihood that we had some situation or a pattern of situations that led to us feeling that something was wrong with us. This is true no matter how ideal one's childhood was. Somewhere along the line, something happened that caused us to believe there were limits to what is possible for us.

Most therapeutic modalities recognize this fact. Traditional counseling frequently seeks to uncover hidden memories that are seen as the root cause of our psychological issues. Then, the counselor brings in the tools of their training to heal the uncovered hurt. Spiritual counselors frequently seek to bring into awareness hidden beliefs from our past so that we can consciously make another choice. Self -help programs such as Greg Baer's "Real Love" program seek to bring into our current life the experience of unconditional love that we missed out on as a child.

There is a realization in all of these means of assistance that no matter how the problem is showing up in our lives, we came into this life okay, something happened to make us think we were not okay, and we need to get back to realizing that we were always okay. Coping mechanisms vary greatly. I can be addicted to drugs, alcohol, sex, or whatever. I can fear intimacy in my relationships and always withhold a part of myself. I can be an overachieving workaholic. I can feel that I cannot follow my calling. Somewhere in all these "symptoms" is the same potential cause: I came to believe that I am not worthy of unconditional love.

What is the way out of this dilemma? The simple answer is to *know that you are worthy and you are lovable*. But how can you truly know that? One way is to receive unconditional love. This is the approach that Greg Baer takes to seek to create environments where people can receive the unconditional love they missed out on as a child. Ernest Holmes says that if we wish to bring more love into our lives, we must be the person who gives unconditional love. By giving love, we attract more love into our lives. Ultimately, it is about reprogramming ourselves to know that in spite of what we came to falsely believe about ourselves, we truly are lovable.

Here is an affirmation I heard recently that conveys this feeling: "You are just going to have to love me because I am so lovable!" Tell yourself that (or something similar) several times a day until you really know it is true and are well on your way to healing your false belief that you are not good enough.

Three-Step Process for Reprogramming Beliefs

Here is a three-step process designed to replace any limiting belief, whether it is "feeling unlovable" or any other false belief.

Step One—Identify the Limiting Belief

Answer this question: *Why do you think you cannot live your life purpose?*

Think on that question and, if necessary, journal on it until you have an answer. Got one? Good.

Now, answer this question: *Why do you believe that's true?*

Got an answer? Good. Take your answer and ask again why you think that's true. Keep asking that question until you believe you have drilled down to a critical belief you hold. Write that belief using the words, "I believe I cannot live my life's purpose because I believe…"

Let's run through an example to give you a sense of how this might work.

After reflecting upon my life's purpose, I have decided that if I was truly being myself I would write books for children. However, writing books for children is not very realistic for me at this time in my life. Why do I believe that's true? I must have a regular income to pay my bills. No one's going to pay me to write books for children. Why do I believe that's true? I don't have any experience writing children's books. Even if I wrote a children's book, some book company would have to print it and sell it so I would have an income. That's just not going to happen. Why do I believe that's true? Because book companies sign up only authors with a publishing history, or those with a very special talent or luck. I have no publishing history, talent, or luck. Why do I believe that's true? I have no publishing history because I have never published a book. I have no talent for writing because my parents told me I could not make a living at it, so I've never tried. I just know I'm not lucky, period. Luck only happens to other people, not to me. Why do I believe that's true? Because my parents told me so.

Hence, the idea that "I believe I cannot live my life's purpose in writing children's books because I believed my parents when they told me I could not make a living at it."

Step Two—Identify the Opposite (New) Belief Needed

Once you have identified the underlying or core belief

that is holding you back, it's time to identify the opposite belief.

Ask yourself this: *What would I believe if I did not believe this limiting belief?* Write that down. Next, ask yourself this: *If I believed what I just wrote, what could I do?* Write that down. Then ask yourself, *What could I do?* Keep repeating the question until you see how you could live your life purpose.

Let's take our example above and apply the steps.

If I did not believe my parents when they told me I couldn't make a living by writing children's books, what would I believe? I would believe I could make a living by writing children's books. If I believed that, what could I do? I would begin writing children's books. Then what could I do? I could be sharing my books with others. Then what could I do? I could be enjoying the fact that others are reading my books. Then what could I do? I could be writing more children's books and putting them out in the world.

Step Three—Program the New Belief

Finally, we must take the vision of what our life would be like if we believed the opposite of what we currently believe and craft a series of affirmations. Effective affirmations carry certain characteristics. First, they must be written from a personal perspective using the word "I." Second, they must be written as if they are already true, as if the experience is already in your life. Third, they must use only positive statements. Avoid the use of negatives in your affirmations. Fourth, it's best to build in some positive emotional experience as a part of the statement.

Staying with the same example, let's write a few affirmations for our children's book author:

- I am enjoying writing children's books and gifting them to the world.
- I am joyfully experiencing pleasure from the smiles of children who read my books.
- Money flows to me with effortless ease as I put my books out in the world.
- I am provided for easily as I write my books.
- Publishers are contacting me asking if they can print my books.
- I excitedly sit down each day to write.
- I am emotionally supported by the people around me, as they see the joy coming through me as I write.

Hopefully, by now you have the idea. There are many resources available for help in writing affirmations.

Once you have some affirmations that strongly resonate with you, pare them down to your top three or so. Write the affirmations on a card. In the morning when you wake up, read them aloud. Before you go to bed at night, read them aloud. Carry the card with you and read them throughout the day. Try to get emotionally involved in reading the affirmations, visualizing them as if they are already true in your life. Whenever doubt comes up, or you hear negative self-talk that argues against your affirmations, simply notice it and let it go. Go back to your affirmations and stay with them. Over time, the positive belief will be programmed. It might take awhile, but didn't it take a lot of time to program the negative belief?

Create a Vision

Earlier we talked about the importance of focusing on the positive vision for humanity's future as a mechanism for bringing it about. Similarly, you need to focus upon a positive vision for your life—one filled with you being yourself and living your life purpose—as a critical aspect of moving you in that direction. Therefore, it's important that you create a vision for your life.

What would your life look like if you were living your passion? What would it feel like? Where would you be? What would you be doing? Write detailed answers to these questions; playing with the words until they are compelling for you. If you are visually oriented, draw a picture or cut pictures out of magazines and create a collage that represents your vision. If you prefer to use words, read your vision each day. If you use a graphic, post it where you'll see it often and spend some time each day looking at it.

From a Vision to Intentions to Goals

Once you have a vision to guide you, your next task is to create the intentions to head you in that direction. Intentions serve as the bridge over the gap between where you find yourself currently and your vision for the future. They are the starting point to lead you to specific actions—the "creation in thought" that must occur before the creation in form can show up.

A list of intentions is simply a set of statements that, when they manifest, will reflect that you are moving into your vision of living your life purpose. Here are a few examples to get you thinking:

- I am writing, editing, and publishing my book by the end of this year.
- I am teaching my children about their ancestors.
- I am cleaning all the clutter from my house this month.
- I am learning a foreign language and will be able to carry on a basic conversation by the end of next year.
- I am attending Toastmasters meetings and learning to speak in public.
- I am eating only healthy food.
- I am exercising four times per week.
- I am completing all my work assignments before their deadlines and requesting additional ones.

Finally, take all your intentions and move them into small, actionable steps. Put them on your "to do" list with due dates—and *do them*! If you find yourself procrastinating or putting other things ahead of your personal-action goals, I suggest that you seek out a good book or training in time management. Stephen Covey's books, *The 7 Habits of Highly Effective People*[32] and *First Things First*[33] are highly recommended.

Becoming Your True Self—and Serving Others

My hope is that you have identified your calling or reason for being, identified any barriers in your beliefs that prevent you from being yourself, created affirmations, reprogrammed your beliefs, and created a vision and intentions to guide you toward becoming yourself. I selfishly want you to be selfish in moving toward being yourself!

I can selfishly desire you to selfishly move toward being yourself because I know that the more you do so, the more selfless you become. The more you become your true self, the more you desire the best for others. You want to give to others in service. You want others to grow and flourish and become all they can become. You want others to become their true selves.

How do we take this "selfish" action of becoming ourselves and move toward becoming selfless and in service to life itself? Let's look at a few steps that may be helpful.

Step One—Cultivate Awareness

Most of this book has been about the first step, raising awareness. In addition, there are two ways I intend for you to develop awareness. Using the ocean-and-wave metaphor from the beginning of the book, my hope is that you are cultivating awareness both above and below the surface of the ocean.

What do I mean?

First, "above the ocean" awareness is bringing into your thoughts many of the concepts and ideas presented in this book. I hope that you stop and reflect upon the words. Weigh what is being said from your own perspective. Determine what is true for you and what is not. Incorporate the ideas I present with your own understanding of life. This allows the model being presented to "come alive" for you. Simply reading through the book is one level of awareness. Reflection, contemplation, and absorption take the meaning to a whole different level of embodiment.

If you encounter obstacles, I offer the reminder that in truth, those outside forces hold no power over you. When your thoughts and beliefs are in alignment with your actions, you will realize your power. If you believe that forces "out there" are keeping you from heading in the right direction, recognize that it is your holding that belief that is the real problem!

This brings us to the second level of awareness, the "below the surface" knowingness. Above-the-surface awareness feeds our intellect and opens us up to deeper wisdom. Below-the-surface awareness allows us to have a direct experience that convinces us that the intellectual ideas are real.

To be specific, I am suggesting that you need to take time to "go within" and get in touch with the sense of interconnectedness that comes when we distract ourselves from the world "out there." To go within is to contemplate, to meditate, to turn our attention to an inner silence.

Each day, you must spend some time looking inward to balance all the time that you are peering outward. Do you have a time set aside each day for going inside yourself? If not, I encourage you to do so. I highly recommend doing this early in the morning, before the day's events have distracted you. Beginning your day by reminding yourself that we are all connected keeps you grounded in love when you encounter conflicts and challenges.

This "spiritual practice" time is essential for all of us, but we don't need to feel stressed over how each of us should do it, or to be concerned that we are doing it "right." I remember, early in my life, studying with others who insisted that meditation could only be done in one particular way. I remember being told that I must sit in a certain posture, contemplate only in a certain way, use only the "selected mantra" that was to be the focus of my contemplation, and follow other dictates that only served to lead me into personal self judgment as to whether I was "doing it the right way." This was an interesting form of Eastern or New Age "fundamentalism," which fortunately I grew beyond. If anyone tells you there is only one way to meditate, politely smile and move on.

Anything you can do to turn your attention away from the outer world of distractions and busyness and inward toward a sense of your true self and your connectedness to the rest of the world is, in my opinion, all you need to be doing. I find that sitting quietly in silence and shifting my focus inward—to my breath, to my sense of inner awareness—is sufficient. The more you do it, the easier it gets. If currently you don't meditate, start with five minutes in the morning of simply sitting in silence comfortably. When thoughts come up, as they always do, simply notice them and let them go. Consider yourself as a witness to your thoughts going by. If need be, you can direct your attention toward your breath, a candle, gentle music, or anything that serves to hit the "pause button" on outer life and take you inward.

If you can, take time in the middle of the day to hit this

pause button as well. I assure you that this practice will serve you. It is like building spiritual muscles. Those that are challenged by anything "spiritual" can simply consider it to be a great technique for eliminating stress.

If you look beyond our outer differences and gaze inward, you will begin to cultivate a true awareness that we all are connected. That deep-level awareness also will assist you in listening to the call to be your true self—to use your talents and gifts for the benefit of others.

Step Two—Growing in Gratitude

As always, you have to start where you are! That is, by having gratitude for whatever you have in your life.

Open your heart and realize how lucky you are, regardless of your current circumstances. What are you grateful for? I find it important to spend some time each day feeling grateful for my life and all that is in it.

If you really knew me, you would know that I live a pretty good life. I have enough money and possessions to live comfortably. I have a wife, friends, and family with whom I share love and affection. I feel comfortable with my accomplishments in life. I have had, and continue to have, wonderful experiences that fill my life with joy. And, I have the fantastic legacy of my grandchildren and my hopes for their lives and their children. Overall, life is good.

Each day I give thanks for a shifting list of things that include many of the following: my life, my wife, my health, my children, my grandchildren, my dog, my house, my possessions, my spirituality, the freedoms of my country, my intellect, my teaching skills, my writing skills, the beauty of the world in which I live, my friends, new acquaintances, the ability to travel and experience different cultures, sunrises, sunsets, the mountains, the oceans, sunlight on my skin, the cool evening breeze, the warmth of my bed, my interesting dreams, delectable foods, interesting aromas, the ability to walk, the ability to talk, and the ability to sit in silence.

Yes, I have a lot to be grateful for—but you can have this sense of gratitude no matter what your life's conditions are. It's easy to dwell on negativity that seems to be staring us in the face. However, I encourage you to take some time each day and turn away from these conditions and toward the things in your life that bring you joy. These can be simple things.

Your body is still alive. You may have health challenges, but you can feel appreciation for the many aspects of your body that function excellently. Each moment, you take a breath. Your mind is still functioning. You are able to read these words. You have the ability to choose what you think.

At a certain level, your needs are met. Yes, you can look at areas of your life where you wish you had more, but you still have things you can feel appreciation for. Most likely, you have access to food and water, as well as shelter to protect you from the elements. You have contact with others.

You are moving toward more human experiences with the potential for joy. You may have had past experiences that were less than joyful, but certainly in your past there also were times of happiness for which you can feel appreciation. You have the potential for happiness in the future. You have the ability to change how you look at things.

The more you feel appreciation for your life and the things that are in it, the more you grow those experiences that bring you gratitude. You get to choose what you wish to experience. Choose gratitude.

The more you choose gratitude, the more you feel gratitude for all the world and all the people in it. The heart opens to everyone. The circle of those that you care about begins to expand wider and wider.

Step Three—Moving from Surviving into Thriving

Building our sense of appreciation for our lives begins to move us out of survival mode. We start to realize that we already have a lot to be thankful for, which by definition means we are not just eking out an existence. If we don't have to worry about surviving, we can begin considering how to thrive and what that means for us.

Maslow's hierarchy gives us a good map for understanding potentially how to shift from survivalist thinking to focusing on thriving. It puts things in an easy-to-understand framework: If our "lower needs" (that is, our physical or animalistic needs) are not being met, they will drive our decisions and actions. It's only when we can move beyond our lower needs that we are able to focus on bigger issues and advanced concerns (that is, our spiritual and metaphysical needs).

Let's look at Maslow's hierarchy or map from three directions and see what insights it might offer us that we can apply in our lives to make the shift to thriving.

First, let's go back in time and consider what our primary motivators were at different points in our life. Right after birth (although I don't really remember it), my physiological needs were, I suspect, primary. I cried for food; I cried to have my diaper changed. In the part of my youth that I can remember, when I was being motivated by my buddies and attractive girls, central to my needs was survival, as well as love and belongingness. As an adult, many of my actions to seek success at work likely were driven by a need for self-esteem. Only much later in life do I have a sense that my primary motivation became a drive towards self-actualization.

Doing this kind of life review to recognize how I had different motivations at different stages of my timeline gives me a sense of how I have evolved in my awareness and consciousness. It reinforces the fact that my life—and all life—is growing and evolving, strengthening that evolutionary viewpoint I have been discussing. It also shows me that earlier in life I was driven by a sense of lack, which I have been blessed to mostly let go of in recent years. In addition, it might show me areas where I still believe in a degree of lack and limitation—where I am motivated by survival. These areas are ripe for personal growth.

Take a few minutes and consider your life and what was your primary focus at different times. Have you been able to move into more "being" needs as a primary motivator, or are you still focused on concerns of meeting basic needs? If you are still focused on meeting these deficiency needs (where you see something lacking in your life), how can you envision your life differently?

Second, let's follow up on that thought by looking at just today—viewing our life in this moment and considering what is currently motivating us. When you wake up each day, do you take time to "create your day" or write to-do list? If so, what's filling your daily planner?

It's important to realize that we have different needs that motivate a variety of actions every day. On any given day, we don't live totally in just one of Maslow's levels. We breathe, drink, eat, eliminate waste, and perform other physiological functions. Most likely we have a roof over our head and enough food to eat. Most of us in Western society are blessed to be living in a stable environment. Although we may not be consciously focused upon it, there probably are some things we do each day to support this underlying level of safety and security. Above these two basic levels, however, things can get tricky.

We may or may not feel that the need for love and belongingness is being met in our life; our assessment of this may be based on whether we have a healthy primary love relationship or a close circle of friends. We may or may not have a healthy sense of self-esteem, depending upon factors in our relationships, our work, our feelings about our appearance, our health, and so on.

As we think about what motivates us each day in all the various aspects of our life, we might consider asking ourselves if our primary motivators come from a sense of lack that we are trying to fill—or if they come from a sense that we have enough or we are good enough, and we are simply trying to give from our abundance and share our unique talents. Which is it for you? The point, of course, is to evaluate our daily motivations so we can release our attachments to deficiency needs and spend more time working on the higher needs that allow us to thrive.

How can we do that? By using the power we have to direct our thoughts and following up with our actions. It starts with the first two steps we've discussed: *awareness*—being aware of where we are focused on "lack" needs, and then shifting our focus to *gratitude*—gratitude for what we already have that will allow the power of our directed thinking to move us in that direction.

A third way of applying Maslow's theory is use the hierarchy to assess our actions in specific situations and see if it offers us guidance for shifts we may need to make. Following are a couple of examples.

First, consider what your underlying motivations might be in your interactions with your primary love life, either in your relationship with a specific person or in your approach to creating such a relationship. When first considering Maslow's hierarchy, it's typical to think your motivation to create or maintain a loving relationship with a significant other comes from the "love and belongingness" needs level —but that's not necessarily so.

In truth, there generally are multiple needs levels at play. You may be seeking or staying in a relationship because you want access to sexual pleasure—a physiological need. You may feel you need the other person's income to survive—a safety and security need. You may believe your friends and family expect you to be in a serious relationship and would think less of you if you weren't—a love and belongingness need. You may believe your sense of worthiness relates to being in a relationship, and that you would be a failure if you were not—a self-esteem need.

In each case, the person is motivated to be in a significant loving relationship, and the underlying need is coming from different levels. There is, however, one similarity: No matter what the level, you desire the relationship because you believe it will fill a lack in you. It's the old Jerry Maguire "You complete me" idea. That belief is simply wrong! You really don't need anyone to "complete" you.

So, what happens if I have a lack that you're supposed to be filling, and then you don't? What if you grow and change? What if you decide to leave me? If you threaten my survival by withholding the meeting of my needs, I might lash out at you. How dare you try to leave me? I need you! Of course, when I think I need you in order to be okay with myself, I am motivated by a sense of deficiency and lack.

The healthiest relationships occur when the underlying motivation comes from a desire for self-actualization. Here, we have moved into "being" needs. We don't sense a lack within ourselves, and therefore don't require the other person to meet a "deficiency" need. We are whole and complete just as we are. At this stage, our motivation is not to get something from someone but rather to give of ourselves to another. We love the other person and want them to live the highest possible life they can. We are there to support them and encourage them and to love them. We are not there to cling to them or limit them in any way. Paradoxically, we have to be okay if they decide they don't want to be with us anymore, because even though it may emotionally hurt us, what is more important is that they are happy and living their dreams. We want them to live a self-actualized life even if apart from us more than we want them to live a limited life with us.

Let's look at another relationship example: People seek out and join social groups such as clubs, organizations, churches, and spiritual centers based on different needs. If you're in such a group, consider for a moment what need is met by participating in it. I know some people who attend a traditional Christian church out of the old-fashioned fear if they don't, they will go to hell—sounds like "safety and security" to me. I know a lot of people who attend churches and spiritual centers because they want to belong to a group where people hold the same spiritual beliefs—love and belongingness. I know people who have gotten involved with the leadership of an organization because it makes them feel important—self-esteem needs.

Although there's nothing wrong with using social organizations as a means of meeting deficiency needs, it is helpful to understand what is motivating your involvement. It can also offer some insights when members of these groups begin disagreeing on the activities they should be doing together. Actually, the most important value that can come from joining an organization is when you do so not to fill a hole, but to give from your abundance. If you are there to be of service to others, to see the group as a means of becoming all you can be, to allow you to sense your interconnectedness to a greater whole, then you tend to bring a totally different level of participation to the group.

I've heard many stories of leaders of social organizations and ministers of churches who come in to express their "being" needs through a desire to grow their group so they can do more good in the world. Soon, they find themselves in conflict with individuals that are resisting them. If these members joined the group to meet their love and belongingness needs and sense that their new leader, in her desire to serve others in the world, is minimizing the meeting of those needs, they may move into "survival mode" and push back. Realizing that members of the group may have different reasons for being there is useful knowledge for the leader that wants to maintain the group.

You might also consider why you work where you do. Is it out of lack, or from a desire to self-actualize and be a force for good for the world? Which do you want it to be?

In addition, Maslow's theory can assist us in moving across the bridge from our physical needs to our spiritual and metaphysical needs, and in seeing how we are all connected. In crossing this bridge, we move from a world where we sense that we are separate from one another and in competition (where we think in terms of "win-lose") to a world where we know we are all connected, and that our highest calling is to be in service to one another-(where we think in terms of "win-win").

Using Maslow's ideas, we gain clarity that our old world is based on a sense of lack and deficiency, where most everyone is focused on these lower needs. In the new world of higher possibilities, everyone is focused on "being" needs—on self-actualization and self-transcendence. Something in us is calling us to make the shift from *surviving* to *thriving*.

Step Four—Being in Service

If you've identified your talent and are expressing it, and have gone through the previous three steps (cultivating awareness, growing in gratitude, and moving from surviving to thriving), the next logical and natural question you are called to consider is, *How can I use my gift to benefit people everywhere?* If that global question is too big, then consider simply, *How will answering my calling be of service to others?* Any service to others, no matter great or small, is contributing to the collective benefit of humanity.

Using your talent to benefit only yourself keeps you in a world where you see yourself as separate from everyone else, where your desire is motivated by lack and deficiency rather than a desire to give from your overflow and to be self-actualized. At some point on your evolutionary journey, you must let go of seeing your life as in competition with every other life and moving to a place where all of life is about cooperation—where you experience the fullness of your life and are called to give from your abundant state of being. To truly live your calling at the deepest level, you know that your talent was provided to you as a means of service to others.

As you begin to truly be yourself and live your life by being in service to others, you have contributed to that key factor that can move collective humanity across the bridge toward a positive future that works for everyone.

Part Five:

Moving Forward in Your Life

In this final section of the book, we will explore the following ideas:

- Everything you have read in this book remains an untested theory for you until you put it into practice.
- Putting into practice the ideas that allow you to become yourself will create a life of joy.
- Becoming yourself moves you forward on your personal evolutionary journey.
- Becoming yourself in a universe where you are deeply interconnected with every other person moves us all forward on our collective evolutionary journey.
- It is time for you to move forward in life.

Putting the Theory into Practice

I hope that you gained some new ideas and some new perspectives on life by reading the preceding pages. I hope that you now begin to see life through this evolutionary perspective.

Even more importantly, I hope you take action to become yourself and, through that, to change the world for the better.

As we move to the conclusion of this book, I want to summarize the *theory* and remind you briefly of ideas presented that you can put into *practice*.

Theory

We are living in a universe that is evolving. Our past has been one where this evolution has occurred primarily in the physical realm. This physical past has embedded animalistic survival needs in us, which have served us in arriving where we are now. Our current and future evolution will occur more in consciousness and the nonphysical realm. We are at an important junction between our animalistic past and our spiritual future. We are being called to greater and higher needs. Answering these needs moves us toward our evolutionary calling.

The current challenges humanity faces are symptoms of the growing need for us to let go of the past and create the space to claim our future. Part of us wants to cling to the past, while part of us wants to move to the highest possibility for humanity. There is a gap between our vision for this highest future and what we are currently experiencing. This gap can appear overwhelming. However, we can build a bridge across the gap and claim our evolutionary calling.

There are three keys to building this bridge—keys that each person can use:

1. Focus less on the differences between us and other people and focus more on our commonalities.
2. Focus our attention on the greater vision—keep our eyes on the prize, so to speak.
3. Become our own true self—identify and express our life purpose.

As each of us uses these keys within our individual consciousness, we shift the collective consciousness toward unity, building the bridge that crosses the gap from our current challenges to a world that works for everyone.

Practice

So, what can *you* do?

As Gandhi called us to "be the change we want to see in the world," this is where you are called now.

Let's review the major ideas we've covered, in the form of a plan of action you can follow. Here are the steps:

1. Develop an awareness of your own evolutionary process. Where do you want to be in life, compared to where you are now? Determine what might be holding you back.
2. Cultivate gratitude—for your life and all the goodness and success you currently have. Build on your focus of gratitude to see those areas expanding in your life. Use the power of your thoughts to imagine those areas expanding in your life. See

yourself making that shift from living in "survival mode" to being an individual who is thriving. Recognize your life purpose and begin living it. By doing so, you will be of service to the world.

3. Develop a vision for yourself and for the world. You do have the power to change the world. What kind of world do you want to live in? What kind of world do you want for your children and your descendents?

4. Create an action plan that moves you into working towards that vision. As an example, you could review the United Nations Millennium Declaration and find an area that speaks to you, that connects to your life calling. Then seek in some way to contribute in your special way to uplift the world.

5. Review the resources in the back of this book and learn more to reinforce the concepts presented here. Share this book with others. Summarize the ideas in your own words and teach them to others.

6. Encourage others to become themselves. As Stephen Covey advised us, find your voice and then help others to find theirs.

Ernest Holmes wrote, "The great are great to us only because we are on our knees. Let us arise. You are the only great person you will ever meet; you are the only great soul you will ever know; within you is the only God you will ever contact. Out of this thing which the Universe has seen to manifest because of Its own nature, with which you and I have nothing to do, comes the future of your evolution—and from nowhere else."

Remember that you were placed on Earth not to play it small, but to live large. You are here to answer your personal call, to empower yourself to be the person you were meant to be. As you answer the call to personal empowerment, you will become ever more aware that everyone is related and all future generations are our descendents. They are calling you, and they are calling me. Let's answer their call with love.

Our Humble Theory Revisited

So, we come full circle and return to the humble theory of evolution presented at the beginning of the book. Let us return to our simple visualization of the ocean and how we saw our sense of focus and direction evolving. However, this time we will expand it a bit. I invite you to return, again...

Imagine, in your mind's eye, a vast ocean with lots of little waves rising, peaking, and cresting above the ocean's surface. The waves rise and fall. Imagine them rising and falling in slow motion. Imagine hitting the "pause" button during this process so that you have a still picture of one moment in time, with all the waves that are cresting at that particular moment. Once again, hold that image. It should look like a vast number of little peaks cresting upward from an infinite ocean.

Now, imagine that each of those waves is a human being. Imagine that each wave can direct its attention outward (above the surface of the ocean) or inward (below the surface). When a wave's attention is focused above the surface, it sees each wave as separate and apart from itself. It notices their differences; it senses their competition. When a wave's attention is focused below the surface, it sees each wave as rising from the same source. At this level, there are no differences and no need for competition. Just like these imaginary waves, we humans have the same choice: to look outward at our differences or inward to our common nature.

Now, staying with this visual, I want you to visualize a sequence of how each wave (or human) is moving through a set of different approaches to how their attention is focused.

In the first phase, the wave's attention is focused outward, above the surface. It notices all the different waves and their interactions with each other. It notices how the waves are interacting with other things in the outer world. In trying to understand all these external interactions, this outward-looking wave may attempt to define numerous unseen powers that seem like gods controlling the buffeting of the waves. The wave sees itself as victim to the whims of these external forces. The wave is in competition with the other waves. It's only ability to control life as a wave is to try to appease these external forces and hope for the best.

In the second phase, the wave's attention is still focused outward. However, in its attempt to understand the external interactions, it has coalesced its story about external forces down to one all-powerful God. The wave is still a victim to this external force. The wave is still in competition with the other waves. It still believes it has no control, but at least now there's only one God to deal with. *If I can get on God's good side,* thinks the wave, *maybe he can help me in my competition with the other waves.*

In the third phase, the wave's attention continues to be focused outward. However, with its growing wisdom, the wave begins to see and better understand how the various external forces play out as they knock into one another. It measures what it sees. It begins predicting with great success what will happen next. The wave begins to think that maybe there is no God "out there." Maybe the key is to learn more about how these external forces work and make better predictions so that it can control life. The wave is still a victim to these external forces, but is becoming empowered by moving into a better understanding of how to use the forces. Life begins to be more about using this knowledge for self-benefit in competition with the other waves.

In the fourth phase, the wave's attention begins to turn downward, to under the surface. The wave recognizes that there are limits to its understanding of the above-the-surface world. There are things the wave can't seem to explain simply by measuring what's going on "out there." The wave begins to realize that even its attention and awareness come from someplace else. The wave recognizes that no matter how successful it is in its competition with the other waves, something is missing. At some point, the wave shifts its focus inward. This change brings new information. Yet, the wave is still mesmerized by the external life. It shifts its focus up and down—above the surface and below, back and forth, attempting to understand what is really real and what is really important. The below-surface sense of connectedness begins to reduce the outer sense of competition.

In the fifth phase, the wave is at peace, moving its attention effortlessly both above and below the surface. It recognizes the value of the outer experiences but is no longer victim to them. Rather, the wave sees its below-surface nature as its real truth, drawing strength from it. It recognizes that it is connected to all the other waves at its source. It recognizes that the interactions of the waves on the outer level are simply an opportunity to gain experience and wisdom via that temporary path of a sense of separation. The wave begins to realize that the affinity (the love) it felt for other waves was simply a force that was moving its attention away from their differences and toward their similarities. The wave begins to realize that this entire process was set up for the wave's growth and understanding. The wave begins to realize that the ocean has embedded within the wave a special purpose or reason for existing. The wave begins to live that purpose, realizing that its purpose is designed not only to serve itself, but also to serve all the other waves and the ocean itself.

At this point, the simple wave moves into an even more expanded awareness—a sixth phase, a new realization. It still can move effortlessly between the experiences of being above or below the surface. It still recognizes that it is connected to all the other waves. However, at this new stage, it recognizes that this connectedness extends both above and below the surface. As it looks above the surface and sees the other waves, it knows that it is looking at a part of itself. The love that has called the wave to allow it to seek its connectedness with the other waves now is experienced at a full level, both above and below the surface. Below the surface, the wave increasingly experiences its inner connectedness to the other waves via pure consciousness, tapping into a sense of "no thing" and "no form."

This is the source that gives rise to the experiences we have above the surface. Above the surface, the wave experiences the unfolding of the evolutionary path it first experienced as separation from the other waves, yet moved into greater awareness of its connectedness. It recognizes that it dropped into this temporary story as an individual wave that began by rising up from the ocean, and at some point will return back to the ocean. It knows that even after it returns to its source, this above-the-surface, larger story will continue as a venue for the growth and experiences of the other waves.

Yet, looking below the surface again, the wave is aware of its own evolutionary growth as it embodies the learning gained from its above-the-surface experiences. There is a constancy deep below the surface that is melded with an ever-unfolding growth within the wave's awareness. Both are serving the wave. Ultimately, the wave realizes that above-the-surface and below-the-surface perspectives are simply different aspects of the ocean of life itself. It is all One.

Everywhere I look, I see other aspects of the Oneness.

It is easy for me to forget that Oneness when I am focusing my attention "out there" on things that may not be going exactly as I desire. Challenges can bring me into seeing that outer world of the waves as being the only reality. I begin to live in fear that I am not good enough, not worthy, that I cannot be myself. I fear what others think. I believe that I have to control life and all the things around me. I believe my "back story" is real. Hidden fears drive my life.

Somehow, I have to let go of the illusion. Somehow, I have to let go of my fear. I have to be all right being vulnerable, knowing that everything is perfect even in its sense of imperfection. I have to be all right with moving within and sensing the connectedness with others. I have to be all right with being seen as my true self—which is not that "outer" story. Somehow, I have to remember who I really am at my source.

There are guides and support mechanisms all around us designed to draw our memory back to this source. Although these guides use different tools, one that we all know about is the power of love, with which we started this book.

It is easy for me to get distracted by physical life and all its demands. Yet, there are those who can stop me when I go down that path and redirect me back to what is important, if I stop and listen. My children, my grandchildren, my wife Mary, my dog Harmony, and others use that power of love to remind me. Those we love can serve to "re-mind" us—to bring our "mind" back to the awareness from which it came.

When I play ball with Harmony, when I lie on the floor and pet her, when I see her expressing joy over riding in the car or playing ball or getting a treat---when I see that smile on her face, that wag in her tail, that joy in her heart---something in me opens me up. That "something" makes me step aside from being separate and apart from her and connects me with her at a deep level. The truth is, we have always been connected—the only thing that love is doing in that moment is moving my attention from the distraction "out there." This feeling of connection stops me from focusing on our differences, our worldly concerns, anything that feeds a sense of right and wrong. It calls me back to the truth: that I am not separate and apart from Harmony or Mary or anyone or anything else. Love is a force for calling me to remember that I am truly connected to everything and everyone.

As we experience love in all its forms---from our relationships, to the joy of nature, to the pleasure of a job well done, to the multitude of ways this experience can move us to place of realizing that this life is really a life "to live for," may we also sense it as that evolutionary force of which Teilhard de Chardin wrote. Love is calling you home to the source from which you came. Isn't it about time you harnessed that force and discovered fire again? It's time to be yourself.

Bibliography and Resources

Following are the resources I used in writing this book. All are books, unless otherwise noted. I've placed an asterisk by the resources likely to be the most useful and accessible introductions for those interested in further exploring the ideas I've presented.

Beck, Don Edward, and Cowan, Christopher. *Spiral Dynamics: Mastering Values, Leadership and Change.*

*Beck, Don. *Spiral Dynamics Integral: Learn to Master the Memetic Codes of Human Behavior.* (Audio Learning Course, Sounds True Audio)

Bruteau, Beatrice. *God's Ecstasy: The Creation of a Self-Creating World.*

Chopra, Deepak, and Mlodinow, Leonard. *War of the Worldviews: Science vs. Spirituality.*

Covey, Stephen. *The 7 Habits of Highly Effective People.*

*Covey, Stephen. *The 8th Habit: From Effectiveness to Greatness.*

*Dowd, Michael. *Thank God for Evolution: How the Marriage of Science and Religion will Transform Your Life and Our World.*

Holmes, Ernest. *The Science of Mind.*

*Holmes, Ernest. *The Essential Ernest Holmes (Jessie Jennings, editor).*

Hubbard, Barbara Marx. *Conscious Evolution: Awakening the Power of Our Social Potential.*

Kelly, Kevin. *What Technology Wants.*

Levoy, Gregg. *Callings: Finding and Following an Authentic Life.*

Maslow, Abraham. *The Farther Reaches of Human Nature.*

Maslow, Abraham. *Toward a Psychology of Being.*

McIntosh, Steve. *Integral Consciousness and the Future of Evolution.*

*Phipps, Carter. *Evolutionaries: Unlocking the Spiritual and Cultural Potential of Science's Greatest Idea.*

Pink, Daniel. *Drive: The Surprising Truth about What Motivates Us.*

Schlesinger, Stephen C. *Act of Creation: The Founding of the United Nations.*

Stewart, John. *Evolution's Arrow: The Direction of Evolution and the Future of Humanity.*

Swimme, Brian, and Berry, Thomas. *The Universe Story: From the Primordial Flaring Forth to the Ecozoic Era.*

Teilhard de Chardin, Pierre. *The Phenomenon of Man.*

Wilber, Ken. *A Theory of Everything.*

*Wilber, Ken. *The Integral Vision.*

Wilber, Ken. *A Brief History of Everything.*

United Nations Millennium Declaration

The following United Nations resolution is taken from this website: http://www.un.org/millennium/declaration/ares552e.pdf

> **Resolution adopted by the General Assembly**
> [*without reference to a Main Committee (A/55/L.2)*]
> **55/2. United Nations Millennium Declaration**

The General Assembly Adopts the following Declaration:

United Nations Millennium Declaration

I. Values and principles

1. We, heads of State and Government, have gathered at United Nations Headquarters in New York from 6 to 8 September 2000, at the dawn of a new millennium, to reaffirm our faith in the Organization and its Charter as indispensable foundations of a more peaceful, prosperous and just world.

2. We recognize that, in addition to our separate responsibilities to our individual societies, we have a collective responsibility to uphold the principles of human dignity, equality and equity at the global level. As leaders we have a duty therefore to all the world's people, especially the most vulnerable and, in particular, the children of the world, to whom the future belongs.

3. We reaffirm our commitment to the purposes and

principles of the Charter of the United Nations, which have proved timeless and universal. Indeed, their relevance and capacity to inspire have increased, as nations and peoples have become increasingly interconnected and interdependent.

4. We are determined to establish a just and lasting peace all over the world in accordance with the purposes and principles of the Charter. We rededicate ourselves to support all efforts to uphold the sovereign equality of all States, respect for their territorial integrity and political independence, resolution of disputes by peaceful means and in conformity with the principles of justice and international law, the right to self-determination of peoples which remain under colonial domination and foreign occupation, non-interference in the internal affairs of States, respect for human rights and fundamental freedoms, respect for the equal rights of all without distinction as to race, sex, language or religion and international cooperation in solving international problems of an economic, social, cultural or humanitarian character.

5. We believe that the central challenge we face today is to ensure that globalization becomes a positive force for all the world's people. For while globalization offers great opportunities, at present its benefits are very unevenly shared, while its costs are unevenly distributed. We recognize that developing countries and countries with economies in transition face special difficulties in responding to this central challenge. Thus, only through broad and sustained efforts to create a shared future, based upon our common humanity in all its diversity, can globalization be made fully inclusive and equitable. These efforts must include policies and measures,

at the global level, which correspond to the needs of developing countries and economies in transition and are formulated and implemented with their effective participation.

6. We consider certain fundamental values to be essential to international relations in the twenty-first century. These include:

- **Freedom.** Men and women have the right to live their lives and raise their children in dignity, free from hunger and from the fear of violence, oppression or injustice. Democratic and participatory governance based on the will of the people best assures these rights.

- **Equality.** No individual and no nation must be denied the opportunity to benefit from development. The equal rights and opportunities of women and men must be assured.

- **Solidarity.** Global challenges must be managed in a way that distributes the costs and burdens fairly in accordance with basic principles of equity and social justice. Those who suffer or who benefit least deserve help from those who benefit most.

- **Tolerance.** Human beings must respect one other, in all their diversity of belief, culture and language. Differences within and between societies should be neither feared nor repressed, but cherished as a precious asset of humanity. A culture of peace and dialogue among all civilizations should be actively promoted.

- **Respect for nature.** Prudence must be shown in the management of all living species and natural resources, in accordance with the precepts of sustainable development. Only in this way can the immeasurable riches provided to us by nature be preserved and passed on to our descendants. The current unsustainable patterns of production and consumption must be changed in the interest of our future welfare and that of our descendants.

- **Shared responsibility.** Responsibility for managing worldwide economic and social development, as well as threats to international peace and security, must be shared among the nations of the world and should be exercised multilaterally. As the most universal and most representative organization in the world, the United Nations must play the central role.

7. In order to translate these shared values into actions, we have identified key objectives to which we assign special significance.

II. Peace, security and disarmament

8. We will spare no effort to free our peoples from the scourge of war, whether within or between States, which has claimed more than 5 million lives in the past decade. We will also seek to eliminate the dangers posed by weapons of mass destruction.

9. We resolve therefore:

- To strengthen respect for the rule of law in international as in national affairs and, in particular, to ensure compliance by Member States with the decisions of the International Court of Justice, in compliance with the Charter of the United Nations, in cases to which they are parties.

- To make the United Nations more effective in maintaining peace and security by giving it the resources and tools it needs for conflict prevention, peaceful resolution of disputes, peacekeeping, post-conflict peace-building and reconstruction. In this context, we take note of the report of the Panel on United Nations Peace Operations and request the General Assembly to consider its recommendations expeditiously.

- To strengthen cooperation between the United Nations and regional organizations, in accordance with the provisions of Chapter VIII of the Charter.

- To ensure the implementation, by States Parties, of treaties in areas such as arms control and disarmament and of international humanitarian law and human rights law, and call upon all States to consider signing and ratifying the Rome Statute of the International Criminal Court.

- To take concerted action against international terrorism, and to accede as soon as possible to all the relevant international conventions.

- To redouble our efforts to implement our commitment to counter the world drug problem.

- To intensify our efforts to fight transnational crime in all its dimensions, including trafficking as well as smuggling in human beings and money laundering.

- To minimize the adverse effects of United Nations economic sanctions on innocent populations, to subject such sanctions regimes to regular reviews and to eliminate the adverse effects of sanctions on third parties.

- To strive for the elimination of weapons of mass destruction, particularly nuclear weapons, and to keep all options open for achieving this aim, including the possibility of convening an international conference to identify ways of eliminating nuclear dangers.

- To take concerted action to end illicit traffic in small arms and light weapons, especially by making arms transfers more transparent and supporting regional disarmament measures, taking account of all the recommendations of the forthcoming United Nations Conference on Illicit Trade in Small Arms and Light Weapons.
- To call on all States to consider acceding to the Convention on the Prohibition of the Use, Stockpiling, Production and Transfer of Anti-personnel Mines and on Their Destruction, as well as the amended mines protocol to the Convention on conventional weapons.

10. We urge Member States to observe the Olympic Truce, individually and collectively, now and in the future, and to support the International Olympic Committee in its efforts to promote peace and human understanding through sport and the Olympic Ideal.

III. Development and poverty eradication

11. We will spare no effort to free our fellow men, women and children from the abject and dehumanizing conditions of extreme poverty, to which more than a billion of them are currently subjected. We are committed to making the right to development a reality for everyone and to freeing the entire human race from want.

12. We resolve therefore to create an environment—at the national and global levels alike—which is conducive to development and to the elimination of poverty.

13. Success in meeting these objectives depends, *inter*

alia, on good governance within each country. It also depends on good governance at the international level and on transparency in the financial, monetary and trading systems. We are committed to an open, equitable, rule-based, predictable and non-discriminatory multilateral trading and financial system.

14. We are concerned about the obstacles developing countries face in mobilizing the resources needed to finance their sustained development. We will therefore make every effort to ensure the success of the High-level International and Intergovernmental Event on Financing for Development, to be held in 2001.

15. We also undertake to address the special needs of the least developed countries. In this context, we welcome the Third United Nations Conference on the Least Developed Countries to be held in May 2001 and will endeavour to ensure its success. We call on the industrialized countries:

- To adopt, preferably by the time of that Conference, a policy of duty- and quota-free access for essentially all exports from the least developed countries;

- To implement the enhanced programme of debt relief for the heavily indebted poor countries without further delay and to agree to cancel all official bilateral debts of those countries in return for their making demonstrable commitments to poverty reduction; and

- To grant more generous development assistance, especially to countries that are genuinely making an effort to apply their resources to poverty reduction.

16. We are also determined to deal comprehensively and effectively with the debt problems of low- and middle-income developing countries, through various national and international measures designed to make their debt sustainable in the long term.

17. We also resolve to address the special needs of small island developing States, by implementing the Barbados Programme of Action and the outcome of the twenty-second special session of the General Assembly rapidly and in full. We urge the international community to ensure that, in the development of a vulnerability index, the special needs of small island developing States are taken into account.

18. We recognize the special needs and problems of the landlocked developing countries, and urge both bilateral and multilateral donors to increase financial and technical assistance to this group of countries to meet their special development needs and to help them overcome the impediments of geography by improving their transit transport systems.

19. We resolve further:

- To halve, by the year 2015, the proportion of the world's people whose income is less than one dollar a day and the proportion of people who suffer from hunger and, by the same date, to halve the proportion of people who are unable to reach or to afford safe drinking water.
- To ensure that, by the same date, children everywhere, boys and girls alike, will be able to

complete a full course of primary schooling and that girls and boys will have equal access to all levels of education.

- By the same date, to have reduced maternal mortality by three quarters, and under-five child mortality by two thirds, of their current rates.
- To have, by then, halted, and begun to reverse, the spread of HIV/AIDS, the scourge of malaria and other major diseases that afflict humanity.
- To provide special assistance to children orphaned by HIV/AIDS.
- By 2020, to have achieved a significant improvement in the lives of at least 100 million slum dwellers as proposed in the "Cities Without Slums" initiative.

20. We also resolve:

- To promote gender equality and the empowerment of women as effective ways to combat poverty, hunger and disease and to stimulate development that is truly sustainable.
- To develop and implement strategies that give young people everywhere a real chance to find decent and productive work.
- To encourage the pharmaceutical industry to make essential drugs more widely available and affordable by all who need them in developing countries.
- To develop strong partnerships with the private sector and with civil society organizations in pursuit of development and poverty eradication.
- To ensure that the benefits of new technologies,

especially information and communication technologies, in conformity with recommendations contained in the ECOSOC 2000 Ministerial Declaration, are available to all.

IV. Protecting our common environment

21. We must spare no effort to free all of humanity, and above all our children and grandchildren, from the threat of living on a planet irredeemably spoilt by human activities, and whose resources would no longer be sufficient for their needs.

22. We reaffirm our support for the principles of sustainable development, including those set out in Agenda 21, agreed upon at the United Nations Conference on Environment and Development.

23. We resolve therefore to adopt in all our environmental actions a new ethic of conservation and stewardship and, as first steps, we resolve:

- To make every effort to ensure the entry into force of the Kyoto Protocol, preferably by the tenth anniversary of the United Nations Conference on Environment and Development in 2002, and to embark on the required reduction in emissions of greenhouse gases.

- To intensify our collective efforts for the management, conservation and sustainable development of all types of forests.

- To press for the full implementation of the Convention on Biological Diversity and the Convention to Combat Desertification in those Countries Experiencing Serious Drought and/or Desertification, particularly in Africa.

- To stop the unsustainable exploitation of water

resources by developing water management strategies at the regional, national and local levels, which promote both equitable access and adequate supplies.

- To intensify cooperation to reduce the number and effects of natural and man-made disasters.
- To ensure free access to information on the human genome sequence.

V. Human rights, democracy and good governance

24. We will spare no effort to promote democracy and strengthen the rule of law, as well as respect for all internationally recognized human rights and fundamental freedoms, including the right to development.

25. We resolve therefore:

- To respect fully and uphold the Universal Declaration of Human Rights.
- To strive for the full protection and promotion in all our countries of civil, political, economic, social and cultural rights for all.
- To strengthen the capacity of all our countries to implement the principles and practices of democracy and respect for human rights, including minority rights.
- To combat all forms of violence against women and to implement the Convention on the Elimination of All Forms of Discrimination against Women.
- To take measures to ensure respect for and protection of the human rights of migrants, migrant workers and their families, to eliminate the increasing acts of racism and xenophobia in many societies and to promote greater harmony

and tolerance in all societies.
- To work collectively for more inclusive political processes, allowing genuine participation by all citizens in all our countries.
- To ensure the freedom of the media to perform their essential role and the right of the public to have access to information.

VI. Protecting the vulnerable

26. We will spare no effort to ensure that children and all civilian populations that suffer disproportionately the consequences of natural disasters, genocide, armed conflicts and other humanitarian emergencies are given every assistance and protection so that they can resume normal life as soon as possible.

We resolve therefore:
- To expand and strengthen the protection of civilians in complex emergencies, in conformity with international humanitarian law.
- To strengthen international cooperation, including burden sharing in, and the coordination of humanitarian assistance to, countries hosting refugees and to help all refugees and displaced persons to return voluntarily to their homes, in safety and dignity and to be smoothly reintegrated into their societies.
- To encourage the ratification and full implementation of the Convention on the Rights of the Child and its optional protocols on the involvement of children in armed conflict and on the sale of children, child prostitution and child pornography.

VII. Meeting the special needs of Africa

27. We will support the consolidation of democracy in Africa and assist Africans in their struggle for lasting peace, poverty eradication and sustainable development, thereby bringing Africa into the mainstream of the world economy.

28. We resolve therefore:

- To give full support to the political and institutional structures of emerging democracies in Africa.

- To encourage and sustain regional and subregional mechanisms for preventing conflict and promoting political stability, and to ensure a reliable flow of resources for peacekeeping operations on the continent.

- To take special measures to address the challenges of poverty eradication and sustainable development in Africa, including debt cancellation, improved market access, enhanced Official Development Assistance and increased flows of Foreign Direct Investment, as well as transfers of technology.

- To help Africa build up its capacity to tackle the spread of the HIV/AIDS pandemic and other infectious diseases.

VIII. Strengthening the United Nations

29. We will spare no effort to make the United Nations a more effective instrument for pursuing all of these priorities: the fight for development for all the peoples of the world, the fight against poverty, ignorance and disease; the fight against injustice; the fight against violence, terror and crime; and the

fight against the degradation and destruction of our common home.

30. We resolve therefore:

- To reaffirm the central position of the General Assembly as the chief deliberative, policy-making and representative organ of the United Nations, and to enable it to play that role effectively.
- To intensify our efforts to achieve a comprehensive reform of the Security Council in all its aspects.
- To strengthen further the Economic and Social Council, building on its recent achievements, to help it fulfill the role ascribed to it in the Charter.
- To strengthen the International Court of Justice, in order to ensure justice and the rule of law in international affairs.
- To encourage regular consultations and coordination among the principal organs of the United Nations in pursuit of their functions.
- To ensure that the Organization is provided on a timely and predictable basis with the resources it needs to carry out its mandates.
- To urge the Secretariat to make the best use of those resources, in accordance with clear rules and procedures agreed by the General Assembly, in the interests of all Member States, by adopting the best management practices and technologies available and by concentrating on those tasks that reflect the agreed priorities of Member States.
- To promote adherence to the Convention on the Safety of United Nations and Associated Personnel.
- To ensure greater policy coherence and better

cooperation between the United Nations, its agencies, the Bretton Woods Institutions and the World Trade Organization, as well as other multilateral bodies, with a view to achieving a fully coordinated approach to the problems of peace and development.

- To strengthen further cooperation between the United Nations and national parliaments through their world organization, the Inter-Parliamentary Union, in various fields, including peace and security, economic and social development, international law and human rights and democracy and gender issues.

- To give greater opportunities to the private sector, non-governmental organizations and civil society, in general, to contribute to the realization of the Organization's goals and programmes.

31. We request the General Assembly to review on a regular basis the progress made in implementing the provisions of this Declaration, and ask the Secretary-General to issue periodic reports for consideration by the General Assembly and as a basis for further action.

32. We solemnly reaffirm, on this historic occasion, that the United Nations is the indispensable common house of the entire human family, through which we will seek to realize our universal aspirations for peace, cooperation and development. We therefore pledge our unstinting support for these common objectives and our determination to achieve them.

8th plenary meeting
8 September 2000

About the Author

Mark Gilbert is a spiritual teacher and writer who lives in Colorado with his wife, Mary, and his chocolate Lab, Harmony. He holds a Bachelor of Science in Psychology from the University of Alabama in Birmingham and a Masters in Consciousness Studies from the Holmes Institute. He supports the growth of spiritual centers around the globe in his role with the international headquarters of the Centers for Spiritual Living in Golden, Colorado. He also is a certified trainer in Spiral Dynamics, frequently writes for *Science of Mind* magazine, and publishes a blog at consciousbridge.com.

Notes

(Endnotes)

1. *The Principles of Psychology*. James, William (1890), ed. George A. Miller, Harvard University Press, 1983
2. *The Triune Brain in Evolution: Role of Paleocerebral Functions*, Paul D. MacLean, 1990, Springer
3. *The Dragons of Eden: Speculations on the Evolution of Human Intelligence*. Carl Sagan, Ballantine Books, 1978
4. *The Study of Instinct*. Tinbergen, Niko. Oxford, Clarendon Press, 1951
5. *Supernormal Stimuli: How Primal Urges Overran Their Evolutionary Purpose*. Barrett, Deirdre. W. W. Norton, 2010.
6. Wikipedia article on "Abraham Maslow".
7. *A Theory of Human Motivation*. Abraham Maslow (originally published in Psychological Review, 1943, Vol. 50 #4, pp. 370–396). Available online at http://www.altruists.org/f62
8. *Towards a Psychology of Being*. Abraham Maslow. Wiley, 1998.
9. *The Secret*. Rhonda Byrne. Atria Books, 2006.
10. *The Intention Experiment: Using Your Thoughts to Change Your Life and the World*. Lynne McTaggart. Free Press, 2007.
11. Wikipedia article on "orienting response".
12. *The Farther Reaches of Human Nature*. Abraham Maslow. Penguin, 1993.
13. From the web site http://www.

integratedsociopsychology.net/self-transcendence.html

14. *Drive: The Surprising Truth About What Motivates Us.* Daniel Pink. Riverhead Trade, 2011.

15. *The 8th Habit: From Effectiveness to Greatness.* Stephen Covey. Free Press, 2005.

16. *The Science of Mind.* Ernest Holmes. Tarcher/Putnam, 1938.

17. *Spiral Dynamics: Mastering Values, Leadership and Change.* Don Beck and Christopher Cowan. Blackwell, 1996.

18. *Sex, Ecology, Spirituality: The Spirit of Evolution.* Ken Wilber. Shambhala, 1995.

19. *Evolution's Arrow: The Direction of Evolution and the Future of Humanity.* John Stewart. Chapman Press, 2000.

20. *What Technology Wants.* Kevin Kelly. Viking, 2010.

21. *The Phenomenon of Man.* Teilhard de Chardin. Harper Books, 1965.

22. Wikipedia article on "Rumi".

23. From the web site: http://en.wikiquote.org/wiki/Rumi

24. Wikipedia article on "Meister Eckhart".

25. *Meditations with Meister Eckhart.* Meister Eckhart. Bear and Company, 1983.

26. Wikipedia article on "Gnosticism".

27. From the website: http://www.enlightennext.org/magazine/j21/bruteau.asp

28. *Built to Last: Successful Habits of Visionary Companies.* Jim Collins and Jerry Porras. HarperBusiness, 2002.

29. On the internet at http://www.un.org/millenniumgoals/
30. World Bank Monitoring Report 2011: Improving the Odds of Achieving the MDGs
31. Christian Science Monitor (December 26, 2011) "Humankind has Made Striking Progress"
32. *The 7 Habits of Highly Effective People.* Stephen Covey. Free Press, 2004.
33. *First Things First.* Stephen Covey. Simon & Schuster, 1994.

www.ingramcontent.com/pod-product-compliance
Lightning Source LLC
Chambersburg PA
CBHW071707090426
42738CB00009B/1694